AF226897

Notes App

notes app

via

Matt Brand

Qualitative Methods

This is a work of collected writings and ideas. The people, names, events, associations, and descriptions within the book's contents reflect the author's perception and creative choices. They are not intended to be read as objectives facts or historical non-fiction and thus, should not be understood as such by the reader.

The author is grateful to Andrew Gallix for the permission to use a quote from the following previously copyrighted material: "Hauntology: A not-so-new critical manifestation" by Andrew Gallix. *The Guardian, 2011.*

Cover photograph copyright © 2020 by Matt Brand
Painting depicted in cover photograph copyright © 2020 by Matt Brand

ISBN 978-1-953523-01-3

Published by Qualitative Methods LLC
www.qualitative-methods.com

10 9 8 7 6 5 4 3 2 1

First Edition

Dedicated to all of the lost and broken note-taking devices of the world, past and present; the incomplete and imperfect

*When you come to think of it, all forms of representation
are ghostly. Works of art are haunted, not only by the ideal
forms of which they are imperfect instantiations, but also
by what escapes representations.*

—Andrew Gallix

Introduction

This book's primary contents were written between the dates of 9/4/18 and 12/08/20 in my iPhone and Macbook Pro's synced *Notes* application. They're taken from a particular note that I created at the start of that time frame, entitled: Free Writing. Since its creation, this note is where I've tended to jot down writing ideas and linguistic nuggets as they've come to me. These have ranged from word-pairings that I found to have poetic elegance, to banal phrases that suddenly seemed to suggest rich double-meanings, to even full paragraphs that unraveled line-by-line while folding laundry or going for a walk. The common thread, though, is that each entry was captured upon its moment of insight, before the brain had any chance to forget it or later fumble the exact wording upon attempted recollection. A rapid imprint was made of each idea before they had time to otherwise grow, mutate, or whither away.

Despite my criticisms and avoidance of most app-based solutions, I must admit that I find the *Notes* app ideal for this use case. As someone who types faster than they write, the app has become my preferred medium for this need to rapidly capture these swift swirls in passing perception. The legibility of the app's typeface is more consistent than my rushed handwriting, it keeps me organized, and it's less cumbersome than a more traditional pocketbook or journal, both which I still prefer for other writing scenarios. The only instances where this application of the *Notes* app has been detrimental is when an idea comes to me while I'm enjoying phone-free time, in which case my solution has been to repeat the idea's words over-and-over in my head until they commit to working memory. Then I simply write the words down once I can acquire a pen and paper, and then later copy those written words into my Free Writing note upon returning home.

Initially, the thought with this Free Writing note—which should technically be corrected to "Freewriting," had I not come to prefer the typo's implications—was that I could later take each jotted idea from the note's log and proceed it along to full fruition as needed, akin to a musician or producer's draft folder of melody ideas and rough song sketches for future albums. On occasion, I've successfully executed this, withdrawing an entry from the note, then transferring it to a preferred, separate medium for editing—like taking a plant from a nursery home to one's garden where it can then be grown to full size and pruned down as needed. However, these instances have become far and few in-between over the past few years as I've spent the majority of my free time putting *Jukebox* together and working on Qualitative Methods, thus I haven't had as much time as before to sit down and flesh out full pieces.

At some point, while working on *Jukebox,* I looked down the pipeline at some other manuscripts that I had wanted to finish. I figured that I might first wrap a few of those up, and then afterward take the contents of the Free Writing note and proceed to flesh-out and mold any still resonating entries, one-by-one, into a collection for immediate publication. However, I soon recognized that such a forced, mechanical process might quickly subject itself to diminishing returns and creative paths of least resistance. Furthermore, I realized that such a strategy would critically fail to address—and instead actually erase—a unique quality of the Free Writing note and its entries. The note can essentially be viewed as a repository of candid linguistic-snapshots depicting ideas upon their arrival, like ephemeral images of my consciousness shaking hands with something beyond it, receiving its parcels at the precipice of the cognitive doorstep. And so, conversely, if I released a book containing fleshed-out, "finished" versions of the note's ideas then it would look more like a collection of staged photos—images depicting what I later assembled with each of the received parcel's contents, yet highlighting nothing about the parcels themselves or their point of reception. It would be less of a collection of candid shots and more a collection of prepared "Say Cheese" scenarios, less of a Saul Leiter photo book and more of an Alex Prager photo book (huge fan of both). With this realization, I suddenly felt that if I were to take each of the entries from the Free Writing note and then craft them into fleshed-out and polished pieces, then it would be akin to a florist dyeing fresh flowers for a bouquet. That is, it would create and highlight additive artifice rather than embracing the organically unique quality of the selected subject. And so, to showcase such a quality, I ultimately decided that I would publish the Free Writing note as-is in its entirety.

Consequently, this book you now hold features what many might call flawed or unfinished creative works. I believe it is ultimately beneficial to openly display such works as opposed to only releasing their antithesis. Personally, when it comes to creative disciplines, I find that so-called *perfect* and *finished* works are oftentimes neither. I have honestly lost count of the number of interviews I've read where fine artists, musicians, and other creators have recollected having to walk away from a work, to throw in the proverbial towel and ultimately tell themselves, "It's done," just so that they can get on with life or start the next project. Such a frequent occurrence, agnostic of artist or creative medium, begs the question: is a creative work ever truly done? And even if it is, can a given work's creator assuredly look back on it, days, weeks, years later, and still think that that work is perfect as it is? From what I've read, encountered, and personally experienced, that is rarely the case. Instead, it seems the more one creates, then the more they ideally learn to trust intuitive measures, the more they learn to be confident enough with their subjectivity, to say that a work is done and then just live with it, even if it may always look or feel like something could be added or changed.

Though still, when many of us embark on or are in the middle of a creative project, we often act as if imperfection and incompletion are not inevitable outcomes. I'm not denying the pragmatism of suspending such realities; on the contrary, I think suspensions of truths may be imperative for creativity, let alone our survival—thinking in particular of Vaihinger's theory of the *Als Ob*, or Adler's and Nietzsche's related assessments of *fictional-finalism*. However, I believe that this adamant denial of imperfect or incomplete outcomes often proves to be detrimental to creators, especially novice ones. It can result in various shades of towering paralysis or endless perfectionism, which ultimately shrink a creator's potential volume of work—and therefore their ability to learn and grow from finishing things. Furthermore, this fixation on the perfect can drive many creators into mazing, self-sabotaging mind spaces, wallpapered with assessments of personal insufficiency, inability, and other distorted, vampiric beliefs. Cultural appraisal and preference for seemingly perfect works certainly only adds to the pressure of these difficult psychological atmospheres.

But I don't think it stops there. In addition to a detrimental effect on a creator's volume of work and thus, their ability to improve over time, I find that a constant fixation on making perfect or objectively complete works will also take a negative toll on the actual quality of a creator's works. What I mean by this is that the pursuit of such ideals tends to favor and negate certain aesthetic qualities in its output. When a creator sets a work's goalposts in excessively lofty targets, then as collateral, the very humanness that initially spurred that work can get frightfully painted over, blunted, or edited out altogether. Inhuman perfection becomes exalted at the cost of embracing human qualities—rough sketch lines get erased, rough brush strokes get smoothed over, blemishes get corrected, and beauty marks get airbrushed. The sleek suppresses the natural. Frankly, in many cases I find this to be a great shame. If we, as creators, are simply existential vessels recording our experienced realities and then composting them into creative outputs, then to hide the parts of the outputs that most reflect our vessel-nature seems to me to be counterproductive and antithetic to our aims. An expression of human experience that ignores or shamefully hides the human certainly misses the purported goal in some regards. It can, of course, produce some very impressive works that are ambitious and astonishing in scope, yet perhaps congruently sterile and neurotic in quality.

Personally, works that more readily embrace and examine this human quality of the imperfect and incomplete tend to interest me more often than those that try to deny it, hide it, or dress it up through grandiose ornamentation. For example, seeing some sparse, rather abstract-expressionist finger-paintings on display in the windows of a nearby kindergarten yesterday brought me much more ponderous head-scratching than seeing images of Hudson Yards' *Vessel (TKA)* or witnessing the *La Gioconda* amidst a packed room of pushy tourists as a young adult in the Louvre. The latter works may have commanded my respect, but the former summoned my curiosity. Those rudimentary finger-paintings made me consider vantages on human perception, the development of natural creativity, and my mortality. They unfixed me from my present, transporting me to existential perspectives, and then left me with both gratitude and lingering questions about my life and the lives of others. Sure, those kindergarten window tableaus might be considered flawed or incomplete by classical measures—they had confusing composition and scale, an excess of unused white space, and generally indecipherable blobs of paint—but they nevertheless provided me with something remarkable that the more perfected or traditionally completed works could not.

The way I see it, displaying works that embrace incompletion or alleged imperfection can offer us an insightful, more humanizing perspective into creators and their creations. By revealing works at initial or premature moments, we can shed more light on the nature of creating itself. It allows us to highlight the idea that spawned a given creation rather than the creator's ability to take that idea and move it along to a satisfactory endpoint. It can also tell us more about the mind of the creator, the preferences and conditions of the fertile soil where a creative idea took root—which topics a creator gravitated towards, which images they kept returning to, which stimuli shimmered through in their daily peripheries. Our historic narratives of creative disciplines tend to focus on the heroics of the creators that could move ideas and creative fragments to culturally-preferable endpoints for our preconditioned digestion. But isn't it also empowering to study the qualities of the ideas and creative fragments themselves?

To bring all the conceptual talk down to a real-world example that might help illustrate this value of embracing incompletion in creative works, I'd like to recall a fond memory from college. One autumn evening during my junior year, I had a date that started at a favorite coffee shop and proceeded to the Seattle Art Museum (the SAM). I had read that the museum had a big Picasso exhibit debuting at a sneak-premiere that night, so I thought it could be fun for the two of us to check it out before the rest of the city and maybe try to get some free wine out of it since we were frugal, underage students. It was a no-brainer once I realized that it was also the first Thursday of the month, which meant that museum admission was free throughout the city as a part of Seattle's First Thursdays Art Walk.

Upon entering the SAM that night, my date and I proceeded to the ticket counter to receive our free tickets. The ticket-woman handed us two First Thursday tickets and kindly informed us that they would permit us to all of the museum's floors and installations except for the sneak-premiere of the Picasso exhibit, which was only available to the museum's annual membership holders. Admittedly, I was a little disappointed about the original plan getting thrown off, but my date and I were in good spirits from the night thus far and still curious to explore the museum in general, so we shrugged at the matter and proceeded to discuss which floor we should check out first.

I forget which route we took after that exactly. I know there was an ascending flight or two or stairs involved, that I remember. And I recall admiring the museum's infamous, neon cars installation from an elevated side-vantage, then maybe hitting a dead-end and turning around on whichever floor we were on. I only have these brief glimpses because I remember that we were all the while caught up in a nice flow of youthful, first date conversation—that novel mix of anecdotes, lightheartedness, and gradual disclosure, where you could suddenly care less about the activity or venue, as you were more interested in just getting to know someone new, someone who seemed to enjoy your company as much as you did theirs.

At some point, I remember proceeding along whichever floor we were on and telling my date a meandering, long-winded joke that would assuredly result in no more than an eye-roll or charitable laugh. After delivering the underwhelming punchline, I remember turning and seeing a painting that looked an awful lot like a Picasso. We approached it to inspect its placard and, sure enough, it was a Picasso tableau. Perplexed, we turned around and realized that we had somehow maneuvered past a velvet-rope checkpoint and queue of museum membership holders while caught up in our conversation, thereby successfully getting into the Picasso premiere! Cooly ecstatic and privately proud, we proceeded through the exhibit in wonder. No free wine was obtained in the end, but a fond memory was created together.

I enjoyed getting to know my date over the course of that evening and can still recall some of the endearing things that she shared with me at the museum and on our walk back to campus. But the one thing that shines the most vividly in my memories from that night was getting to see some pages from Picasso's sketchbooks. The exhibit had featured an extensive collection of the artist's canvases and even included some of his sculptures as well, but it was the pages from his sketchbooks that blew me away. They were unlike anything I had ever seen in a museum before—the incompletion, the lifting of the hood to show the artist's process, that feeling of, "I see where he was going," or even, "Maybe I could do something kind of like that if I tried,"—it was all astounding. The sketches weren't as flamboyant, colorful, or fully-formed as some of the surrounding tableaus in that room, nor did they need to be. Their more bare and undeveloped quality made the art feel human, and the artist, like an approachable, creative friend showing you some doodles, rather than like an unattainable, monolithic master on display in a center of classist curation. Even today, having been lucky enough to have seen some of Picasso's most famous tableaus around the world, nothing has left a mark on me quite as much as the sketches under the glass in Seattle that October night. It remains a formative memory in my informal creative education, affecting how I view others' work and my own to this day.

If I had to boil it down, I would say that there are two things that I find valuable about the displaying of imperfect or incomplete works like Picasso's sketches. First of all, I find that doing such readily instigates more catalytic outcomes than the displaying of perfect or completed works. As an unsure, budding twenty-year-old at the time, seeing Picasso's sketches had suddenly led me to feel like his awe-inspiring level of creativity and skill might be approachable, even achievable in some regards. That can be utterly paradigm-shifting to experience, especially for the many impressionable young minds of the world, or the even larger amount of people who are intimidated or downright doubt-ridden by the mere thought of attempting to create something. Showing stripped-back or incomplete creative works can inspire people by revealing a stepping-stone within a previously inscrutable process. It behaves similarly to an episode of *The Joy of Painting* with Bob Ross or a paint-by-numbers kit by illuminating intermediary parts within a work instead of only serving up the intimidating whole. Observing these provided points in a creative process can help people see how a pyramid in Giza was just single grains of sand combined over time, how Seurat's *Un dimanche après-midi à l'Île de la Grande Jatte* began with just one average dot of paint, or how numerous chart-topping recording artists' careers were preceded by busking a forgettable cover song or practicing to a metronome for hours on end. Every seemingly unachievable creative feat can be broken down into unremarkably achievable pieces—that is what these imperfect or incomplete works remind us. It's a humanizing yet provocative idea, and I think that to encounter it as a layperson is more readily motivating and catalytic than to only see a heralded masterpiece at its end-point where one is more likely to conclude, "I could never make that…"

Showing imperfect or incomplete works can help us beneficially deconstruct creative processes, but I think it can also help us beneficially deconstruct something else—the creators. That is the second key value that I find in the displaying of such works. Just as Picasso's sketches made his abilities seem more approachable to me, so too did they make the man behind them appear more human. They reminded me of my friends at the time, of things we might have doodled while daydreaming during a dry lecture that semester. Not everyone has painted something like *Guernica*, but practically everyone has sketched at least a doodle or two in their life. Some Picasso doodles may be a league above many of our doodles, but the artist is nevertheless getting revealed in a moment of lower-stakes play. Modest, bare works like these help to bring their creators down to a relatable level. It allows us to see these celebrated luminaries in a more relaxed and carefree light, one that typically differs from the highlight-reel depictions shown in textbooks and retrospectives. It would be like seeing a supermodel in their favorite baggy sweatpants and frumpy t-shirt for a day of lounging at home—they probably still look very pretty or handsome, but likely in a more at-ease way than when they are stoically posing on the catwalk in heels and an expensive, angular, avant-garde suit. Ultimately these encounters show us that even the most talented, celebrated creators are still human like the rest of us. This vantage replaces a vertical hierarchy with a horizontal plane, shining the spotlight on common humanistic denominators more than unique and lonely ambitious zeniths, thereby muting the over-accentuated heroics in which culture and the spectacle of the celebrity-complex anchor themselves.

These early or partial works can help us deconstruct creators in another way. Not only do they make creators more relatable, but they also expose their thinking to us. These works can reveal some of the initial ideas, intuitions, and recurring themes on a creator's mind, which might otherwise get covered up in a more completed work. For example, if a writer turns in a first draft to their editor, and it contains a specific idea repeating over and over in the same wording, then the editor's subsequent feedback might advise the writer to reduce the number of times they use that wording or else replace it with synonymous language. From an editorial point of view that would be perfectly logical, but from an investigative standpoint, it would be removing a breadcrumb trail that could otherwise inform the reader of what was most on the author's mind in the first place. I'm not necessarily proclaiming that we should all publish first drafts of texts or ignore our editors. But I am saying that doing such a thing can help expose us to an interesting perspective on what the creator is readily thinking of, what they are plagued by in their daily life. Such a perspective can only benefit us since it allows us to understand more about a given creator and the variables that sparked their creation. I find it akin to when an interviewer asks an artist who their influences were. It may be a trite question, but its answers provide aspiring creatives and art-lovers alike with the ability to trace that artist's lineage, to connect the dots and do the homework in order to see how that artist might think and why. This helps the aspiring creatives by allowing them to perceive and create more like the artists that they admire, and it helps the art-lovers appreciate the artist's work more by better understanding its context and intention. As both an aspiring creative and art-lover, I find all of this to be priceless and again, rather humanizing.

With that, there is one last thing that I would like to note on this topic, and it has to do with that word—*humanizing*. I don't suspect that I'd be making a controversial leap if I said that if something is *humanizing* or possesses a *humanness* to it, then that means that it reflects a human quality. If that is true and I keep saying that incomplete or imperfect creative works are humanizing, then it must also be true that these works reflect a human quality. But which quality would that be exactly? Well, at risk of sounding like Thomas Aquinas or Alexander Pope, I think it might simply suggest that to be human is to be imperfect and incomplete. Surely we can each categorize a fair portion of our lives into moments of strife, feelings of insufficiency, aspirations for improvement, or desires for resolution before we kick the cosmic can. Whether these instances are attributable to an underlying causality or just our cultural and economic pressures, are they not describing an experiential state of incompletion and imperfection? If so, then perhaps the enjoyment that I find with imperfect and incomplete works is, at least in part, tied to their ability to bring us face-to-face with our human nature, in comforting recognition. It's almost like the opposite of an uncanny valley, where seeing a creation's executive flaws causes us to see its humanness and associate with it more.

Witnessing a staggering, completed masterpiece can bring us to a place of admiration—an admiration for an individual's ability to get closer than most to touching conceptual perfection in the realm of aesthetic representation. Whereas witnessing an imperfect or incomplete work can bring us to a place of recognition—a recognition of our shared human experience of struggle and experimentation. The former highlights our desired fruits of success—an outcome achieved by some—while the latter highlights our on-going trial and strife—a process experienced by all. More crudely, I would say perfect works attend achievement and ego, while imperfect works attend shared conditions and embraced nature. Both types of creative works are transcendental in that they can take us to vantages that cause us to reflect on what it means to be human, but I guess I often prefer the latter's tendency to more readily approach the everyday and every person in that transcendence. It understands creative expression as liberated and universal, spotlighting an inherent, creative capacity possessed by all instead of the exclusive, refined mastery possessed by few. This view of creativity leads me to curiously wonder things like, "How might that neighbor I just passed, or the stranger at the bar, or my friend working at the café this morning draw the new apartment complex on our street?" instead of only, "How might Salvador Dalí draw the new apartment complex our street?" Wondering that about Dalí might help me to perceive more like him or further my drawing abilities, but wondering the same thing about neighbors, friends, and strangers can lead me to be more empathetic by examining how those around me are feeling and experiencing life. That kind of exercise helps us to become more empathetically connected and grounded in our communities, to see the perspectives and better understand the value of those around us, instead of tunnel-visioning in on celebrity-culture's exceptionalism or our atomized pursuits. If that trade-off is not important for our sustained existence and survival as a species, especially in the current epoch, then I honestly don't know what is.

Hopefully, some of this prolix rationale in defense of incomplete and imperfect creative works might ultimately help us consider the possibility that such works are, in fact, complete and perfect. The previous Aquinas-like position suggested that humans are inherently imperfect, but perhaps a quasi-Buddhist response would counter that humans are actually inherently perfect, and that we just fail to see it due to our cognitive ability to conceive of a loftier perfection, which we subsequently sublimate into faulty desires in the material world. The benefit here is that these desires can fuel ambition, but the tragedy is that they can sometimes prevent us from seeing the beauty in the way things are. I think this might be occurring with the incomplete and imperfect creative works under current discussion. For example, one person might look at Paul Cézanne's famously unfinished *Route Tournante (Turning Road)*, c. 1905, and after seeing all of its white space and exposed canvas, they might think, "What a shame, it would be better if he had completed it." However, another person might view the same tableau and instead start envisioning what Cézanne would have painted in the blank areas. Or maybe that person might even think, "I actually prefer it this way. It allows the painting to breathe and gives its scene a surreal, dream-like or half-there quality, which might otherwise be lost if the painting had been completed."

With the latter person's more open perspective, the tableau's incompletion behaves in an inviting, gestalt manner. It leaves room for the witnesser to complete the work in their mind, to congregate with it. It is as if these works keep an open chair at the table and invite the mind of their witnesser to sit in its vacancy. It reminds me of things like architecture, graphic design, and dub music—intentional meditations on negative space. Maximal or "perfect" masterpieces might leave little room for the witnesser; they make exhaustive use of their real estate, everything is air-tight. Imperfect and incomplete works, on the other hand, leave open space; they pose questions to the witnesser and leave room for their reply, rather than only providing an eloquent, declarative statement to be comprehended. They invite dynamic discourse instead of offering a static monologue.

In the spirit of this notion, I wanted to leave the same open space and invite the same dynamic discourse with this book that you now hold, so I have published the entries of my Free Writing note in their entirety to display them in their own spirit, so to speak. To embrace the incomplete and imperfect, I wanted to release ideas as they had arrived to me, at their various stages of potential "completion," rather than instill my usual amount of hauntological negotiation upon them over time. The intention was for this to serve like a textual sketchbook caught in amber, showcasing the seeds of creative writing instead of its nurtured and pruned flowers. And so, for this text, I simply "extracted" the collected ideas that I had logged into the Free Writing note in my *Notes* app and then committed them to printed pages, like removing cells from a live Petri dish, then staining and trapping them between glass. I removed the ideas from the illusory infinite openness of the digital plane where perfection and sterility are often the goal—if not the operative working conditions—and then imprinted the ideas into the calcification of a printed page, submitted into time and its passing.

Prior to print, I simply gave the extracted text two rounds of spell check for any obvious typos, separated the entries with a standardized dividing line, and prevented any awkward divisions, widows, and orphans between pages via indenting as needed, even if that meant having some unbalanced spreads as collateral. Otherwise, the text is essentially untouched—odd punctuation choices remain; ideas that now read illogical, stupid, or perplexing to my present self were left in; and single-word typographic widows and orphans were not treated with hanging indents or adjusted tracking. The outcome is a work that is theoretically closer to the initial point of creative conception than anything else I have or likely will ever release. There is the least amount of hauntological negotiation between farm and table—more of a direct in-line from my mind to yours, shortening the distance and reducing the obfuscating layers that otherwise result from standard revision and editorial processes. In *Jukebox*, I examined hauntology through its application in the related forms of music and poetry, observing how each transacts through its practitioners—both authors wielding the past and witnessers summoning that past into the present—as they seek therapeutic relief. Whereas, this current book looks at hauntology, not as an asset of creative forms or a synthesis of their recreational consumption, but rather as an adjustable variable that is inherent in the negotiated development of practically all creative ideas and their *executions*—what a perfect word for this context.

In that regard, this current book owes dedication to the author César Aira, who famously doesn't edit his work before he publishes it. Without a doubt, that approach influenced some of my thinking on this current text and its release. This book must then also be dedicated to my very dear and exceptionally well-read friend, Elin McCready, who first introduced me to Aira's work during an unforgettable late night of tasty fish dishes, countless beers, and pivotal conversations at a favorite izakaya in Nakameguro. Simply the best. Love you, Elin!

Free Writing

the date of the change is getting closer
you want it to be perfect
to cast the next chapter like an award-winning film
to ensure the ingredients for sweeping romance, memories, excitement,
growth are all there
you remember that much of it is all through chance and seized moments
and that simply moving into it will welcome the possibility of the next
world to you
so you say 'fuck it' and 'yes'
and you go through with it all
just to see what might be waiting

———————————

i forced myself to forget you
despite your sharpie outline
your highlighter aura
your face and skin colored in with childhood crayon
your flashlight smile

———————————

celebrating the ill
we televise and pay and ask for more of them
we digest images of the ill
and metabolize them into a desire to replicate the same
unaware that inside the unmet 3-D reality of the image
at the time of its creation, was a scene of vapid stillness and anxiety
that would be met if ventured towards

celebrating the ill
similar to celebrating the dead
as i suppose it becomes an ultimate point on a cycle which everyone
reaches
one way or another

———————————

i've said hard goodbyes to beautifully-hearted women at train stationed
hotel fronts in various countries
i've felt inspired to make my own art from ingesting the various forms of
amazing art created by others
i've offered my love and selflessness to those i meet, replicating the love
and selflessness given to me by family and those i've been intimate with
along the way
it is all a way to continue the perpetuating way of the world

———————————

i listen to my strange music
it makes spaces and novel shaped pools for my mind to swim in
and wander around
one such pool is house shaped, one is night shaped, one is kiss shaped
my mind swims and moves between these pools
i think of you
waking up around this time on the other side of our slowly dying space
habitat
i love the smallness of your lips, how delicate and mine they feel when my
larger mouth and lips dance with them, leading, pulling and teasing out
their follow
i think of the big lush tropical leaves around the area where you live

the sound of your voice speaking russian words i don't understand at a
novel velocity of peculiar phonemes creates one such pool

———————————————

It was the small details that made me want to move to that city… the
artist who tattooed me playing Amon Tobin and being in a long-term
relationship with the drummer from an acclaimed math-rock band I liked
in high school. The casual cafe bar that Yannik and I grabbed a beer at,
people working on laptops in the homely light in the late hours. The
complete lack of pretense in the techno clubs on a Wednesday night.
Club mate vodkas.

———————————————

an angel delivers our drugs

———————————————

maybe heaven is a dance party with those whom we've met throughout life,
i certainly hope so

———————————————

write on the idea that Stephen Hawking said humanity only has 200 years left to live

———————————————

jokes told in movies

ancestor to internet memes
jokes told in movies
we'd recite them at cafeterias, parties, in AIM chat windows
a way to assume common knowledge and shared taste in humor
to relate and display,
interstitial crutch for flirting or laughter

but more, unbeknownst a way to connect
to the time, culture's movement
the unwavering organic machine
we became a part of it
keeping spirits alive and building new
breathing human material through them;
extended life expectancies,
time outside of itself, multiplying through use of its byproducts.

but it seems different now;
reduced to infrequent occasion, we recite them over drinks,
when reconnecting with the people with whom we used to frequently
exchange them, out of a habit or memory i suppose
but all in less frequency, less readiness,
something changed between then and now.
sure, the internet,
but that's outside of us,
what changed within us?
maybe it's another case of the inevitable,
the shedding and going further into some sort of precise identity
seeing how much was just filler or clothes that we assured looked good
and fit right on each other

box office sales meanwhile dwindle
is it that we've replaced the things we so adored, so leaned on in youth
that through our technology we desired ourselves to be the creators of
that thing, to subconsciously bring it closer to ourselves?

———————————

something went wrong one time and so I can't write that way again

————————————

the effects of holding someone in your heart outside of real time
decision, loyalty to a principle or religion against the flow of being
and the changing tide of offerings

————————————

Deck of 51

————————————

don't you realize
this is all there is
the habits to make fruit
the habits to kill crops

————————————

a future where the world evolves back into tribes
where monarchs are all cultural icons of art and celebrity
their followers, fans who are moved by the belief
that deep appreciation and experience of the artist's work
creates inherent differences between them and others
only to be awoken by the fact that even amongst themselves
their differences in perception, relation, and value to the artist's work
are personalized. ultimately resulting to an eating or murdering of those
they worshiped.
great artwork ensues.

———————————

"you've probably unintentionally broke someone's heart, you just haven't
realized it yet"
"you've probably unintentionally broke someone's heart, they just never
told you"

———————————

thank god for steve roach
he said, yawning off a day's private torments
ridden in guilt and, if he weren't so tired, frustration that he didn't achieve
as much as he would've liked today

is the machine broken
is the machine learning

thinking of a play palace
thinking of the 90s
and retro-futurism in houses i'll never experience
so untouchable, the ghost of a ghost
it makes the fantasy even more tantalizing and dreamlike
(is this why people get into vintage pornography?)
the idea that people felt or thought differently then
that there is a hidden treasure or wavelength only accessible in that time
frame
i suppose in a way that's how it all is, hericlitean waters

o accessible gateway
make me a prism
taking and exchanging light
into an extrapolation of itself
in other waves to communicate

though too, if it is not too much to ask
let me see how trivial and repetitive
it may be against the larger tale of history

———————————————

visibility of antiforce and protesting power

———————————————

evil as a pragmatic vehicle
to be occupied by that which you are antagonized by,
though which, in turn, ultimately is an inherent part of you
or the limitations of your agency

———————————————

oh how the pleasure will get me
nothing, nothing, nothing
the gunshot of a trivial race
announcing a beginning and an end
in its stationary post as the agents
move themselves in relation at will

———————————————

sade with someone i don't love

i felt like the bad guy listening to sade in bed
with someone i don't love
the smooth jazz melodies no longer felt transportative
but perhaps kitsch, or worse, false in communication or relation,
love songs and longing songs wilt
to cautionary songs, futility songs
true, a flower is dead when it is first defined as a flower
but i take name as the planter

———————————————

private worries,

———————————————

universal consciousness vision felt like normal vision and occupying space, but different, upside-down, not weighted in the eyes, and heavier. the feeling of recalling places and map points from dreams, places that don't exist, recalling them to memory and feeling like they just occurred or are occurring right now in parallel or overlap. That they are a real place, or *the* real place, realer than what was going on in front of you.

———————————

financial insecurity, environmental degradation, media addiction, corporate dominance

———————————

50 polite or sadistic acquaintances can't be wrong

50 polite or sadistic acquaintances could be wrong

———————————

deep-sixing (term for disposing of or destroying)

———————————————

The desire for multiple realities (ascending time)

———————————————

Laura Branigan's version of Self-Control comes on at an unknown
altitude
air travel and train travel help me think
there's something deeper that happens
the detach, the abandon of the routine
of course heaven is in the clouds,
up here one has perspective, occupied omniscience;
i can't help but feeling a deeper love for those i know
a near manic awareness of the long-ball, where it looks like they're
headed,
seeing that their minor tragedies will end

———————————————

Unless i travel to Europe for work in the next 4 months, this is the last
time I'll fly across the Atlantic for a trip in the foreseeable future. I'll have
moved overseas. What will the brain taste be on that next flight; what
will the phenomenological flavor be; will i be grounded in a sensation
of my pure excitement, enthusiasm? Or perhaps my apprehension, and

realism recognizing the new challenges that will await—making friends
again, navigating a new culture and language, redeveloping disciplines
and independences. Will it be sobriety over the big changes happening—
exodus of the corporate route, a new journey into self and my passions,
the common themes from my childhood to present, perhaps conversely
an appreciation for the very corporate routines which felt so deadening to
my spirit—were they, like limitations on a creative project, the very thing
that pushed my creativity and drive against the daily constrictions they
imposed. Perhaps my heart will think of the potential of meeting another
there, especially as someone who in recent years struggles to identify
places where I might meet a partner with shared interests.

I feel an overwhelming outpouring of love for my coworkers along the
way, for the people I've collaborated with and endured the waves with.
For my parents and their help giving me a place to live during the past
year of sacrifice for savings, for my friends for just being there along
the way. I have not married or had a child, but perhaps this is the closest
to that—the focusing and exalting of something that feels altruistic,
personally just, and deeply existentially important sub specie aeternitatis
all finally coming to fruition, or rather, to a deeper more serious stage of
maturation and commitment after resilient perseverance and sacrifice.

One feeling was clear above all others, intuitive certainty. I was on the
path, continuing further up the hill in its timeless spiritual imagery. The
end wasn't near but at least I knew I was progressing on the right one and
with that could remember to savor it as it happened; the end may never
come and even if it did it may turn out empty, underwhelming. It was
these strange unique moments on the path, the unique vantages to the
valleys, the previous inclines, and the horizon further casted, that were
the rewards. I put a song on, closed my eyes and exhaled, feeling it all
happening. Being there, being in it; being alive.

———————————————

lying still at night with the lights off
eyes closed falling asleep feeling how fragile it all is
somewhere else others are already asleep
somewhere else others are in dream narratives
somewhere else others are dying in their slumber
it's all happening, so soft, so alive,
so natural, so inescapable.

---

window seats

Blow a wish with no lips
Trace a fate with origin ink
dream the dream through the train window screen
remember the truth job and feel, really feel, the horse;
beautiful, ready, perfect

the passing nature seems suspended when it does its job
remembering yours and your private power,
you are ageless, taste of destiny.

---

italo disco on the train to piedmont
a big polite fuck you to the more defined and virtuosic in a field
a warm dance, eyes closed, with and for
any who realize it's in the action and voice
that most things important are transferred
inspiration, access, simplicity at cast
unknowns, nobodies, seeds in a storm
good luck, it was fun, come what may
unknown hits and hits by unknowns

———————————————

fall asleep upon me on a train
dive down the alleyways
push at whim into the unfamiliar bars
taste the vermouths, the amaros, the alien liqueurs with me
as we people-watch and discuss and debate the oddities of life
and our minds take secret photos and smell memories of it all
take a dance with me

———————————————

dogs were blue, we just couldn't tell
i started my day talking to you
you, on the other side of the world, going to bed when i'm waking up
moon to my sun, sun to my moon
i was getting over another sinus infection
my energy was diminished, i missed strength and productivity
and perhaps other measures of vitality and a full life that i had fallen for
i hadn't been in the gym for several weeks and missed it
but knew i would likely be back once healthy
that always happens, remembering
that nothing is permanent, movement and change begetting and
furthering themselves
remembering days and years and other forms of measurement were just
that—agreed upon forms
to help facilitate, to help make sense of what in actually, was just a
singular endless string of unraveling events and results
think of how silent, how nearly inexistent, it must feel from space.
if bacteria had media would they experience the same degree of drama
and theatrics as us, falling in love with each other,
evolving in perpetual misunderstandings and unnecessary involvements
you sounded like a shape of a ranch style home
or a black and white photo of brutalism
or a color-washed photo of a pueblo. i guess it didn't matter either way, it
was all slowly but certainly approaching a foreseen end place
which ultimately made you want to ooh and aah at it all,
the great big show

———————————————

hanging out listening to music and chatting
splitting a bottle of cheap wine or vodka
taking turns going into her bathroom to key a bump
so those we didn't want to share with didn't know
i remember it was always awkward when one found out, and you played it
off in the obvious coked out way

i remember her cat she loved so much, always matter of fact, popping up
here or there without much awareness of others or any sort of plot.
the last time i saw her she was in rehab up here, got addicted to painkillers
and never told me;
turned out every time i had ever hung out with her she was high on them;
my paradigm did uncomfortable back-flips.
i was glad she was getting help, and that neither of us were in los angeles
any more.

———————————————

a digital photo made up of moving ants
the dance was changing again
a forming wave on the horizon
hoping it'll be benevolent
hoping it'll be manageable
dreamplaces and untouched landscapes
astonishing heights in nearby shadows
outsides of novel bars, partially lit streets past dusk
viaducts and routes home out of reach
there was someone here we were supposed to find again

———————————

complex folding headphones

———————————

Yahoo! Answers: will you get sick if you are intimate with someone
nearby who is sick

———————————

Code smell

———————————

I charge my smart phone so I can keep using it and
Continue to get to be emotionally involved with people in the exhaustible
new languages of relating that I wouldn't have otherwise
If you have less languages it limits the variety and qualities of emotional
planes we can coexperience
And if emotion is tied to excitatory movements
And excitatory movements to novelty
Then maybe it's already done
We just want more novel coexperience
As the planet dies and capital moves quietly like armies training in the
night

———————————

Lately talking with friends and strangers
alike
about how bad things are getting
Feels less like old dystopian sci-fi plots
And more at home like a broken window you don't have the money to fix
It makes days colder, and invites the real in
So that pain and the hidden
Feel progressively more like a facial scar
Where the only other option now would be a mask

Does being comfortable with the broken and uncomfortable make you
feel smaller or bigger?
Me too.
I'm glad we can at least relate more

---

experiments in attention
attention experiments

Truth and dare

Rules and atmospheres

Sometimes it feels like life has just been a collection of witnessing
cautionary tales

Sometimes it feels like the lives of many I've met have been cautionary
tales, including my own

____

Sunday

A big feeling day
So much that it affects the physical world
My body turns inward, emptying bathtub of water, underwater cave
realizing itself as the earth's plates shift further
Bubbles and whirlpools happen
I feel realistic emotions wage war innocently against dreaming emotions,
as they must
The way the universe has to expand, or living things consume other living
things to survive and further an experience of reality
I wanted to paint wildflowers tonight but I was too tired and fell asleep
with the lights still on, something I'm growing more worried about, more
accustomed to

____

However it ends at least there'd been
A promise in discovery of pollen and its maturing towards a finitude
Honey covered tongue, honey stained eyes
Honey drenched mind nights afterward

In a world or an afterworld
That a breeze or scent may happen upon us, a mystery song wiggling
secret air through the surrounding atmospheres
As a free flight back to the island
Of a feeling or a realization
A complex palace of corridors and mirror rooms
Underneath the linear guise of place and event
And to what end, it is nothing of matter

———————————

Ugly people beautiful cacti

———————————

Archaic shape presences
Invisible star body becoming

———————————

Everything changes
Gratitude is a plasma snake
My socks are polka-dotted
When would I buy polka dotted socks
I forget what I am
So I can become something different
We need a better word for loss, or lack even
Look at a mountain
Look at a mushroom
Look at a cloud
It's already different
Air tight illusion
Stealing your love
Your joy
Your possibility
With such subtle askings of permission

———————————

Smell of amusement parks before I was old enough to understand money
Fixed amounts of human fossil fuel - love, memory, attention, devotion

———————————

A feeling some hand stole,

____

Everybody a different bridge

____

water flowing elsewhere (dissonance)

water flowing elsewhere
you back by your foreign ocean
me, a river, look at me,
where am i flowing into?
i guess that's what this is all about.
having eroded much over long time towards
a hope, a dream, a lake or inland ocean
before knowledge of water flowing elsewhere
untouching concurrent dreams, longing
to merge, against nature
a blubbery human flesh pressed against the flat glass of time, space.
the thing that hurt
wasn't so much the thing itself:
pain, change, ideas
but the painting it constituted:
alternatives, inability, war against memory, against emotion
altitudes of the chest, pressures of lungs, the diaphragm
changing uncertainly

———————————

creatures from home

———————————

What's my new comfortable
Clad sheets, casual discussions obliged
Grow old and into it or change and calm
Maybe it's always been there, like earth or stupidity
Maybe it's right or wrong, or a wing above
I don't know, it was nice just going with it
Touching, talking, being with and around others
Life wasn't the bastard child everyone told you it was
I knew that before I finally went to bed towards 6am, as much as I knew I
might second guess it, come awakening
Which is why I wrote it down now

To See

Behind the camera
There's less magic, less car image
Than you'd expect
And yet there's still something,
Even for coffee eyes; something
So lavender honey, so encouraging.
So you keep doing it, to see.

———————————

The heart is a beautiful guide
Dodging you through the infinite streets, bars, international alleyways,
rich peaks, lonely valleys, and doorways of the world

———————————

In the day time everything looked so perverse
Incorrect, uncomfortable or sad
In the night it suddenly all looked perfect
Exactly what was needed

In the day all looks perverse and imperfect
In the night time everything is essential and beautiful

____

Fragile passing moments of rich gratitude

Passing moments of gratitude
As fragile as a cherry blossom in rain,
Rice paper on a tongue tip
As a sun sets a thin sheet of light over the periphery

____

The daytime hawk
The nighttime salamander

____

Childhood, when the interior walls of the soul are painted

One of the beauties of no WiFi was when you're on the top of a foreign mountain feeling the sacred smallness and seeing the big picture inside your head in a car ride back to the city you're staying in
When you want to text someone that you love them, you can't, so instead you put it on your heart, like another sacred layer of mâché or a warm scarf of found foreign silks

----

Descending into the Kathmandu valley at night you see the millions of lights, mimicking a night's sky. Diving back into the divine heavens of humanity.

Top of mind examples of me being a daft idiot:
Thinking Céline Dion wasn't good
Thinking *The Alchemist* must be overrated

I used to think cameras were stupid and that my eyes/brain would capture everything I needed. Now years after getting into photography and loving cameras, I still, in a funny way, relish most the moments where the instance is all too beautiful (regardless of if you don't have right lens, camera, whatever)

Emotions
Crying important tears listening to Steve Roach at night in the back of transportation driving you back from a mountain to a city in the foreign valley.
Warm rich tears coming from a deep red exotic cavern of the soul, twisting like a cosmic fractal, tying to everyone else's in hidden inner-space.

with Nepali wood carving, Indian marble inlay

The motion of life is: returning
Returning from summits
Returning from heavens, from deserts, from islands
Going back to the earth; back to others, from where we first came.

———————————————

There's no such thing as timing
Good or bad timing implies it can be improved upon or that it's not
already perfect
If we were seeing what was happening instead of trying to bend it
towards an attached onto idea of "should be happening" then we'd save a
lot of emotions and sadnesses

———————————————

Even former unpleasant recurring dreams or irrational fears later seem
just indifferent breadcrumbs that led you to where you needed to go

———————————————

So much of life, or our job in it, I think, is just setting things in motion.
A farmer plants a seed. A doctor dresses a wound but the wound heals
itself. You decide where you need to go and your heart will take you there.

———————————

Cloud

Airplane tilt
Flattening horizon
Back into the mist
Between places
So much undeclared
So much, to be left
So much, to return
Changed map

———————————

There is a very potent and important magic in ordinary things. A lot of
people just seem to miss it while searching for the occult and saviors.

———————————

Player Piano

Soul is stationary
Time and event are a closed loop moving over it

Baddie in a Honda

Epicenter of a feeling

Catch the space

____

The messy solutions

____

New List

____

forced sunrise

____

softwork

____

dripped in rain

The documents

DJ Rest of the world
World's rest

I know I'm almost 30
And that my skin still smells neon
But you sound just like a planet
And you pull me back to you when you speak like a glass of wine
And I want you forever, every night
Toothpaste touches, whispered feeling;
You're in my alone-silence like a prayer
And I want all the lights to go out except your candle
Me and you alone at any cafe
Like nobody in the forgotten library at the end of the world
Wrapped in scent-memory and fabric softener
I think that would be alright
That would be alright

———————————————

I think I'm at my most sexually attractive
When pushing two carts alone through the tall corridors of an Ikea's
retrieval warehouse, after the showroom, before the check-out
Because it is always during a moment of renewal, surviving and working
through complex emotions and devout lonelinesses, barely keeping it
together at moments, almost puncturing through the scar tissue to the
base support layer of the memory foam, steps before a cash register so I
can go to a prelude to a home and put everything together again

———————————————

"maybe you're right," as you roll over
turning to look into yourself, before sleep washes you new again

———————

Friends of culture

———————

Relaxing Obsolescence
Calm Obsolescence

———————

Call me instead

———————

Customer

____

Soft shirt

____

Strange and fateful

____

weird whisper
a weird whisper
more approximately
intelligent labels
paid to distract each other
free teachers

____

paying postage to send each other imprints in time, unique codings to take into our own, to mutate us mutually—the rare music tape on acetate, the genetic and climate encodings on a bottle of wine, the same of a bag of roasted coffee from around the world. We want to experience the digestion of code together, desiring to evolve through the same experience and time remnants into more advanced future selves; to escape ourselves but not alone.

———————————

Things perfectly not our own; the cute strawberry stands appearing and manifesting much as the fruit they sold, a small and sudden bright red in spring, and charming in how they keep to themselves. The intonation in everyone's pronunciation of "tchüss," with its inherent sweetness, kindness, which to those saying it may otherwise just sound routine, commonplace, like nothing at all. It reminds you of how beautiful the mouths of people moved in France, creating, stressing, unstressing in a foreign and hypnotic way unlike your own. Or the way that the people in India would bobble their heads side to side for agreement, like a sideways nod which somehow looked and felt even more pleasing, more agreeable than the nod motion that you're accustomed to.

———————————

"There's room, space," stranger in foreign accent scooting over at the urinal trough below the international pub in 2019.

Being back in Europe reminds me of its countries' histories, holding
many more generations and their learnings which could perhaps be said
to contain that many more lessons and acquired wisdom compared to
the US. The latter's degree of capitalism always felt a bit adolescent to
me with its inherent obsession of bullying, virility, distractions of self-
imposed competition, and trying to get away with things without getting
caught. There seems to be a very active mindset of 'outsmart or be
outsmarted,' resorting to a 'every person for themselves.' I didn't like the
taste of it... it felt like high school, people acting into roles while secretly
still filled with fears, confusions, envies that they later come to realize are
empty or pointless, and perhaps too often by the time they do, it's too late
to actually enjoy the damned thing.
Europe in comparison seemed to have somewhat more collectivistic
behavior (not entirely of course, and not to ignore its own issues that
it faces on the topic, but more than the US at least), young-adulthood,
middle-aged.

Airports and ikeas

In America

In America it'd be shit to die in a small budget airplane after they just charged you an extra $50 at the gate when your baggage couldn't fit in their company's dimension-restriction cell, detailing what you can and can't take with you. They say in a way it's your fault from beforehand. And in a way I guess this is how it goes for a lot of us.

Exactly, we met in a town by a lake just when winter was horror flick trailering
Mirrors were outlawed ages ago there, part on account of the lake, part on account of the inhabitants' history.
'Natural law,' mouths joked, smile snugged.
Maybe that's why we joined eyes like dogs because time doesn't come and go or fly or start, I remembered; that last song was by... oh it doesn't matter, here's another to build off it: funny how we always manage to find and redress a trope we sold off when we were younger- receipt for shared cake, details for ikeas and airports and movies; all the better for it.

I send pointing arrows to mistook friends

———————————————

Hey sorry, I just got to this hidden speakeasy in the department store
because I was told you found some people like me, do I use my coupon
here?

Sorry, I don't mean to interrupt your work
It's just that I got to this speakeasy corner
In this department store
Because I was told there'd be other shoppers like me
Song tag, geo tag, quote tag, price tag
Yeah, I don't like it, but the other stores were closed and it's getting late
So I'm worried this may be my last chance to get wardrobe right for
tomorrow's pageant

———————————————

Exchanged heart coupons,
What a way to know and agree
The big sale on the sky and we're lucky because the walls are glass

Landmark and regal hand mistaken for true music
I try to keep my habit of sending arrows to those shaped like undefined
planets and cosmic bodies,
Saying the museum brought you to an air and this was the closest thing to
an updated jar, how's work? Or this ambient song was ambiguous enough
to feel safe late at night; do you feel safe late at night? I'm reworking a
safety thesis, I hope you might like it. If not you, someone else.
I understand comic characters with bright red and yellow who frequent
air bubbles like bars, how it looks like they're smiling in the panels after
being matter of fact with another character. Neither seemed necessarily
better for it but it makes me remember the comic better, makes me relate
and want to read more.

———————————————

Sometimes all it takes is a cup of coffee and a forgotten song to soap-
water and paint yellows, peaches, scarfs through the sky

———————————————

Why do we all get so scared of gently passing our inflatable truth globes
in the sun, why the need for a hand

As some of you may know

Systems

Joanie's new tattoo

---

we always hide in plain sight

I revised my hope
A blind woman in a boat towards an unknown shore
Now a blind woman in a boat towards an unknown shore, where only
part of the boat is trustworthy

———————————————

'It's like when you move to a new city,'
She motions with her hand towards a cafe window behind her, to
encapsulate all that's beyond it
'After months, a year, two, the novelty and opportunity vanish and it is
just another mental cubby occupied by a collection of routines, knowns,
and expectations. It's not bad I guess, it just leaves me to feel to discern
between a boring happiness towards death or a secret battle against
domesticating, wondering. But I mean, at my strongest—if I should even
call it that—I remind myself that if I acted on that wondering it would
just lead to the same or a similar lot not that long after... so perhaps it's
less work to make due with what I have? It's very poignant and, like,
appropriate isn't it?'
'How so?'
'I mean how we're perpetually having to allocate more and more time
and energy throughout our maturations to tend to the immaterial fields
our minds create, all the while feeling at best apathetically content with
a perpetually sinking ship. I just thought it felt like a microcosm for the
bigger shtick at hand, like with the world. I don't know. Anyway, that was
a lot. Yes, I still love him. Marriage is fine. So what's new with you? How's
the new life thing? Tell me everything!'

———————————————

44

It could've been there
But it had to be here
I didn't know why
I was just asked to steer
Dancing blind by my heart
Eyes closed from the start
Foot after foot through
Year after year
I could still be there
But I'm glad to be here

____

She'll never forget the feeling
leading up to her engagement

after she sent the pitch-deck for the special day
to brands who would be interested in her reach

waiting eagerly for their reply
hoping they might say yes

____

To go and reach and find
It wasn't what I thought it would be
Still
To help identify a better next
It helps

————————————————

thank you for giving (sending DMs to DJs who've created something that was beautiful to you)

heart is paint and i wet mine into words with water
i wrap my words in a tear ball
and roll them over to you
'thank you for helping us feel'
light string-canning in hopes to give some back to you
and note this down to help continue it with others

————————————————

i have a weird thought
in dreams and drunk moments
away dormant, blue still, perfect in an unnatural way
miami, los angeles, barcelona
somewhere not itself in the future maybe or else
driving, walking, loving, witness
who do i give this to;

is it mine, or is it a message
i think that's one of the biggest questions
for us to ask quietly
and answer fully
(esp. if we've seen enough to know);
answer it then

———————————

nyctinasty

———————————

You do your part in the rain
A few petals make a frame
And suddenly it makes sense

———————————

I don't want to say it in this age
But a moment at the grand worker's steps reveals everything.

———————————

The trickster
Comes to town
A hole with arms and legs
Swallowing everything up apathetically
Leaving the onlookers to themselves

———————————

Mortality integration

———————————

He was touching too much infinity
And I knew it might return in the wrong car later down the road

———————————

Ask me all questions, tell me no lie

———————————

dating fatigue
lack of motivation to travel
either i'm getting reclusive
or content; maybe both

———————————

Granted an existence where
At best I can ever
half know myself
half know others
half know the world and its workings

———————————

I thought of the beautiful, engaged models
The coke we had done and how we were all talking
over each other to say how much we like each other,
thinking how long this or any of these things might last

———————————

Sometimes I like to sleep alone on the couch
Away from the bed and its reminders
I remember reading an art historian's thoughts of a Muncht exhibition,
commenting on the prevalence of the bed in his work,
noting that it is typically where we enter and leave the world, the place of
both our ecstasies and our sufferings, our communions and our solitudes;
our nightly lofty fantasies and our grounding illnesses and injuries.
A couch was more indifferent, more uninvolved and therefore freeing.

———————————

making cold brew coffee by eye
putting my finger in the dirt of my houseplants to figure if they need
water
walking home rather than biking, more time that way
bullshitting over a beer with a friend
meeting someone new
accidenting a canvas into a better fate

———————————

shuttle hit the trees
first as bird then end of time
consciousnesses outer spiral off again
soft place emptied like coffee bean
why walk and drool a way into a turning star
books and juries for both walls

____

crying on trains heading home

____

we each had to relearn the importance
of willingly losing the war on loneliness
to get back to anything that ever mattered

____

a time when everything in life was more clear for what it was
all the curtains were lifted but the sadness of a curtainless world was gone
and was replaced by a respect and admiration for everyone
in our different positions backstage

____

feeling a weird sort of seasick
on planes away from feelings
back to routines.
when is it enough
to dance into a chance
only you and music can say for sure

The only thing I had left of you was the forecast for the city where
you live in my weather app, in a weird way it made me feel I was still
able to approximate how you might be feeling; to still have a thread of
connection between us.

Clean comics

One of those people where the majority of their personality could be
surmised through what they wear.

Nature continues

Deposits of freedom

The truths that everyone hides
And the spaces that allow them to work with those truths
And the spaces that allow them to feel safe sharing them
And the spaces that welcome them to reveal themselves

Humans, the creatures that hide in light;
scared of plain truth, its awkward angle when held up against time's air-
magnifying mirror, glaring telescope

Instead of saying I love you
or I don't know what I'm doing
or we're all dying, you
see the way
others recoil the same
So you learn to change truth sounds into mute motions

A long hug at the airport,
An extra kiss goodbye at the hotel,
A mouth on a wound,
Soft unguarded eyes and gentle smile after mending with an old friend,
A hand on the shoulder of an acquaintance feeling the weight,
Silence until it moves you

[or]

Spiegel im Spiegel

Humans, the creatures that hide in light;
We were scared of plain truth, its awkward angle when held up against
time's air
Magnifying mirror, glaring telescope

Instead of saying I love you
or I don't know what I'm doing
or we're all dying, you
see the way
others recoil the same
So you learn to change a mouth into non-verbals

A longer kiss goodbye at the hotel,
A mouth on a wound,
A soft unguarded look and gentle smile after mending with an old friend,
A hand on the shoulder of an acquaintance feeling the weight,
Silence until it moves you

____

An Ending

I remember holding her as she cried into my chest
It was one of the most beautiful and perfect sunny days in the world, as
we stood by an oversized pool at the island resort
She told me that the couple next to us at lunch was video-chatting with
their 4-year old daughter in her mother tongue
They told their daughter 'mommy and daddy have to go but we love you'
In between sobs she told me she had never heard that from her parents
I just held her and kissed her head

Minutes later I bawled my eyes out under my cheap sunglasses on the way
to the airport
It was one of the days when I saw that there wasn't enough love in the
world

I knew months later things might fall apart between us due to distance
and its strains and that that's just how things go
And that that pain is the important thing

I thought about her when having sex with someone else weeks after she
told me she didn't want to communicate anymore
And then the week after that when lying on my couch alone

[or]

An Ending (Where the property meets the sand)

I remember holding her as she cried into my chest
It was one of the most beautiful and perfect sunny days in the world, as
we stood by an oversized pool at the island resort
We had had lunch at its beachside restaurant where a Russian couple next
to us had been video-chatting with their 4 year-old daughter back home

She told me that they had said 'mommy and daddy have to go but we love
you'
Her sobs entered between words as she said she had never heard that
from her parents
I just held her and kissed her head

Minutes later I bawled my eyes out under my cheap sunglasses on the way
to the airport
It was one of the days when I saw that there wasn't enough love in the
world

I knew that months later things might fall apart between us due to
distance and its strains and that that's just how things go
And that the pain-dancing and shining lights through all of this is the
important thing

I thought about her while having sex with someone else weeks after she
told me she didn't want to communicate anymore
And then the week after that when lying on my couch alone

———————————————

She reversed herself like a pillowcase for washing
Her eyes opened
She said -I'm bound to be this way, it's who I am; my mother hates
herself so why can't I?
The rain looked plain and everywhere
Outside the hotel lobby
She said - Maybe I made the wrong choice; I always make the wrong
choice. Or at least I always make choices and allow myself to think they're
wrong.
Luggage moved past us, some stayed at nearby tables with drinks and
silhouettes
About

———————————

A passing of clouds
then

Less after time
though they perhaps of benefit

Wetter landscape, pristine and possible
Focal and directive

Then the barren and self—
Desert, island, mountain, valley
What else

What else. You think
In a foreign city older

You, it,
others after

Best to be with it

———————————

you were going along just fine
until the truth memory was plastered
up against the front wall again
above the eyes, below your dream-hope

———————————

a recently expired stranger jet-streams
confessions to me in a hotel room of shared taffies
we invent an even economy of songs off youtube for the day
i enjoy when people make agreements
always a way of negotiating time and awareness
like here we were absorbed in a capsule
ignoring the outside world, or how we would repackage the day
after over-thinking it or feeling
a readjustment to standard time the day after

———————————————

Well, I Hope All Is Well.

———————————————

I met me
a dream to say, you'll say
in a future you with
backwards yous in stream
you parade
in twos, you met you
youing again

———————————————

Headstart

I'm almost 30 and experiencing my first crush on someone in a long
time. I forgot what it was like to feel nervous about a date, or that it's
even possible to still feel these feelings. So I stay in tonight and lie on
my couch late at night listening to Hope Sandoval's voice with my eyes
closed, just feeling it all. I don't need any clever wordplay because this is
poetic and perfect enough.

I don't know what age it was when I first started getting enclosed in time
capsules. It'd always be at a café, a window seat on a plane or train, alone
on the couch late at night when the world is still. A song would come
on or a visual memory would bubble up from years ago to make sure
it wasn't overwritten. My eyes would do the thing with water where the
massive complex system keeping you alive yields exhaust to feel more
in the big vast atmosphere that somehow created it and somehow will
eventually take it back. The eyes lock on a fixated point that often has
nothing to do with the memory—a piece of asphalt before the cafe
in Berlin, a couple strolling in Paris, the blank living room wall—and
everything else around dulls; it's not in the capsule. Perception of time
changes and you stew. I don't know what age it was when it first started
happening, but it's happening more and more lately. And I think that's a
good sign.

———————————

your face's lightning over
i'm a jack-o'-lantern
happy and scared

———————————

and i'm wind in trees
every clock ends at
tears into smoke
again

———————————

The feeling of someone coming back alone after an unsuccessful date
to an apartment that they had cleaned and tidied in hopes of bringing
someone home; in their best clothes, looking in the mirror (describe that
feeling in a piece, how the clothes/apartment image intensify it)

———————————

Adults can still have crushes, I learned that when my heart felt like it was defibrillated upon our eyes meeting in the German class you taught. You smiled and I smiled and our bodies didn't exist; age was a forgotten joke, space a fake advertisement.

———————————

A million people have written a book called 'my crazy life'
And still it helps

———————————

if your christmas list asked
for glow in the dark bedroom ceiling stars,
a bright lava lamp, obnoxious day-glow clothes;
dreams, belief, a journal, warm limousine church candle,
eyes
i am a form, then
open accepting ink

holding with
two hands under armpits like a cat
myself to an arrangement of mirrors
i am a long-lasting flashlight even if naked or wrong
if your foot is in the dark

———————————

i already bought the things i needed to buy
and sold or outgrew them all
i only needed love now

———————————

I reached a point in my life where I didn't want to exorcise the internal cathartically through terminalless dancing, joyrides, and corporeal expression. I wanted to do repeated but eternally novel feeling partner praxis where we get wine and I look into your eyes like maybe you are the end of the world and "where to?" and "I don't care" on this cliffside because what else and that feels right, and that feels good. And a pop song starts.

Fuck, I'm out in the world and I see different aspects of what I'm attracted to everywhere. And you're the only consummate of them all in one. Who ARE you?! What gives you the right to walk into my so carefully constructed bullshit life like this? This all sounds stupid and trite and like maybe this is the way it's all meant to be, naïve 90s R&B, obvious Prince song. But it was there on all the drugs with a friend at the gay party in Berlin that I realized I really like you and wanted to surrender my time and the influence of the direction of my life to you. I didn't have a good reason why, and I guess that doesn't matter.

Going out and getting drunk and such feels like indulgence into a distracting alternative reality. Do more work to reap the results you most want in this one.

———————————————

I softly cried a few tears in my bed after a night of dumb broken partying
because I realized that I recognize my future self calling me from you and
that I had to go into it all...

———————————————

i wonder how you'll feel about me
when you hear and see that i'm one
of those people who is moved so much by music
drifting in and out of times and feelings

———————————————

when I look at you i don't see age
only energy attracting my own
energy that has seen acceleration and slowing
excitements and let-downs
and still exudes itself all the while

———————————————

They said, "Here you can be anything."
And she said, "I just want to be high," and laughed,
as someone put a different song on.

———————————————

Confusing, hot, and then rain
[or]
Bad, hot, and then rain

———————————————

songs for a sad world
Chansons für the triste

———————————————

Food Poems

———————————————

Gratitude for the person
Whose awful exhaust smelt like fart
That took me to lines in carnivals
To elementary school classrooms
To movie theaters
To long commutes home thanks to whoever the anonymous asshole was
To long commutes home when I was the anonymous asshole because I
was too broken and exhausted to care
Thanks for taking me
I almost forgot

----

south moon roving
listening to Prince and thinking of you
the fan blowing air on me
alone in my space after a nap
worried perhaps pleasantly, no, importantly
about where i move my body, where i plant my soul

[or]

south moon roving
listening to Prince and thinking of you
the fan blowing cool air on me alone
in my private space after a nap
feeling whelmed and softly
worried perhaps pleasantly, or, importantly
about where i move my body, where i plant my soul
i want to cry for no reason or every reason
i don't know, am i crazy for this or suddenly simple

this whole crazy movie may end, as the world
and suddenly that's maybe not so awful
that is to say, it'll be okay in whichever way

———————————————

A lot of people wanted to be desired
I just wanted to be.

———————————————

Diurnal

———————————————

I think we now find ourselves in an era in which any science fiction work,
must I think, at least in an quickly metaphoric capacity, turn back towards
habitation on earth, focusing on its inhabitants. Where any other course,
to me, seems escapist, misleading, and betraying to the understood goals
of the genre.

Protists

Your love is like a deep flower
Hour by hour
Hour by hour
Hour by hour

my back sore from the needed posture
at the sushi restaurant, we smiled and cheers'd
faces of pleasure and joy
taking photos in between each perfect poem of taste
in high definition
i would, years later during a cold, be doing dishes
after i quit the bullshit career
and, looking out a new window, think
that there are people who will only know supermarket sushi
and think it's the best damn sushi they'd ever had
and they'd be right.

being afraid of each other is a way of being afraid of ourselves

she asked us
should i 'new phone who dis' him
or tell him to come over

Being afraid of each other was just another way of being afraid of
ourselves. After dinner we all got drinks and she asked us if she should
'new phone who dis' him as revenge for when he ghosted her last week,
or tell him to come over. And I realized that while closing myself off I
had been creating mystery and attraction but preventing room for shared
intimacy, for vulnerability and trust. The things I wanted the most, that
were most natural to me, ended up being things I was inadvertently safe-
guarding from myself as some weird, maladaptive, sabotaging prevention
from being too myself… love was weird. We told her to just have a
conversation with him instead.

i realized that while closing myself off
i created mystery and attraction
but prevented room for shared intimacy and vulnerability and trust; the
things i wanted the most, that were most natural to me, ended up being
things i was safe-guarding from myself in some weird maladaptation from
being too myself. love was weird.

I'm a 1990 American-made model of human being
You can tell from my hardware, worn and factory tattooed

———————————————

we turn off the lights or candy swim
to play with our own minds
they turn like a wind
morning isn't enough

———————————————

Everyone wants a system

———————————————

Charli XCX's episode of My Place on YouTube

The party-zone
Enter catalyst
Evolution epicenter
Temporary ecosystem for development
Temporarily open for construction

indifference is a very cancerous position. What starts off as a benign, innocent, natural response slowly overtime leeches the host's time and agency until something much larger has amassed as consequence— something that, unless identified, may be too large to be resolved within their mortality.

———————————

watching something intently, it moves slower.
this is how we return, and go into a thing
when reality is being watched it tows us with it
back from our unrealities and pulling farces
devil's television, paradise screens.
the realer acid trip; better selves

———————————

Sky is sky blue
You're sky blue too
Look at us truth-building in the same self-music
What a wonderful farce
Stocking of things I didn't know
I needed like houseplants, like experience

____

i cried at the kitchen table tonight
nothing dramatic or cathartic, just pure and real.
i had just finished making breakfast for dinner
listening to an old david bowie interview about why he moved countries
i sat down to my plate of eggs, avocado, and tortillas
listening to 'Heroes'
as i open an email where you detailed fun plans for how we can spend
time together this month
i never had someone do that before.

____

the skinny girl tilting a wineglass nearly the size of her head to her lips
making a smile with her colleague for a photo

____

A broken glass in light shines bright
Or
A broken glass in light shines with clarity

———————————————

Erotomania (excessive sexual desire)

———————————————

I looked at some of the friends I had and became increasingly
disheartened by the fact that the most interesting thing about them, or
at least the only thing they seemed to talk about anymore, was quickly
becoming what they chose to spend their money on. A friend in
industry-x would vent to me on the phone about how they aren't happy
with their job, feeling guilty about it then sighing and sweeping it under
the rug with a blanket statement that they repeatedly try to convince
themselves of, like, "Well, at least it's still kind of helping people," before
spending money on a vacation where their spouse would pick the top-
rated restaurants from brand-sponsored travel blogs so that they could
come home raving about their "authentic experience" or be the kind of
person who when you mention a country in any context must insert,
"Ah yeah, we went there once." And it was likely no inconspicuous
coincidence that each of these destinations was a widely harped location
du jour for experiential-consumerism marketing, often undergoing more
and more gentrification, more and more instagram photos as a result.

Just an increasingly vapid amalgam of corporate office small-talk topics—
the latest restaurants you tried, the vacation you went on, whatever novel
cultural spectacle like the new Netflix show or the upcoming music
festival. Maybe the problem was with me for wanting something deeper
or less empty, less sad. Maybe I was in the wrong place with the wrong
people.

you didn't forget
to be nowhere
jet stream window-washing a feeling
fresh pomodoro red health
nothing disappeared
construction finished, fast cars changed but still go somewhere
and god, how the still mysterious breeze flirts through the leaves
like a vanishing curtain or song of summer.
what i mean to say here is it's never after midnight
trains don't stop, crops of smiles aren't endangered
the metaphysical shape of your favorite toy sings through
as a hot whistle in key
night song, dream bird, friend meal
plain instrument in the abandoned museum
linen, olive tree, reality, endless soil
even after one's years of fires
of petroleums,

a you-thing color as a station
the way the radio dial feels,
beautiful reflective, timeless but promising of an unknown future
chrome high fidelity fiction
round and familiar, round and cyclical
top of the stations, back down to the former
fixed yet changing in programming
attached to a larger car in agency against weather and forces
where to park, where to drive,
but what station
a doing or not doing
against earth, understanding approximations of area
or else just going, ending up a somewhere of definition
you leave the dial for awhile just to see if you might start dancing
to see how it affects the pedal
to see what comes on next

————————————

On vacation with friends, in a passenger seat in a perfect state of
vulnerability and clarity
Passing a neon sign in a foreign country reading "all you need is love"
And feeling the oncoming happiness of acceptance and renewed comfort
Until a second line of neon lit up below saying "and food."
Cheated again
So desperate

————————————

Intervening nodes

Light bird song
Spearhead piercing time's acquired convenience
A strange warm sky gives a golden half sentence
And says finish it in forearms and earth
The clay and sand weight of created clauses and causes, we the
tendered machines making common brokenness into individualized
beauty
Oil canvas signatures on motions and commitments in space
All of us
Invisible brand stitch
Seasonal color ways
7, 9, 10 year intervals
Wax seal vows
Wine grape's character
Signature melange
Child dancer's behavior
Star and organelle
Face of step, face of touch
With no need to manifest into object's
Attempt at objective
Everything laid in its place
To finish it in forearms and earth

———————————————————————

Googling if people ever eliminate temptation
Googling how to stay in love

Liberating words
Liberating meanings
Liberating people

Science is catching up to truth
And marketing, even faster
Hopefully the former beats the latter
As its language is now the trusted dialect for business decisions
Though both easily subverted and missing the point

A danger of the attention economy is that attention is an equalizing
bioforce with fairly common limits
Thus superseding intelligence-
Taking away the power of those who know better or could otherwise
help or warn others

"If you control the menu you control the choices" - Tristan Harris

Favorite distortions

Language and story-telling are just tools for shaping perception
And ultimately I wanted to use them in ways that attempt to contribute
toward the listener/reader's growth and asking of questions
Rather than their use and giving of money/loyalty

(from India)
Iyer season in India, everything is in the streets here, as he said
You walk down one and you are in the middle of life
Colors, scents, sounds; people, animals, children, death
India was an endless list not of destinations but concurrent ingredients—
the hundreds included in the old royals' paan or a rich dish of spices

There is something powerful in the form of a list
The greats like Whitman and Brainard nailed this with anaphora
I felt it all then in the back of a car whizzing through the Kolkata rain
It was that rain
It was the narrow avoidings of collisions with other vehicles and
pedestrians
It was the pleasant dampness after a long hot day
The relief of presence after the tyranny of a day's labor
A list is a prayer
Stringing emotions, adding them into larger cumulative emotions
Drops begetting puddles
Begetting oceans
Begetting mist
Begetting tears

———————————————

inspirational sleeping

lay away, alone or in an afternoon with another
self spirit lifts when the factory is closed
conjuring images of the possibility, of the dream zones
reach and kiss them, feel the feeling of a future self
continue the interesting path for interesting blisters

____

we can build a heart

maybe we can build a heart
i know i have a zephyr dream and you,
a stomach-garden's need,
but maybe this could last forever
a flying bathtub for two
extended outer and inner space tours
enough words to exhaust future's library,
even the wild plainness of time and developed familiarity

____

look, i don't know how time works
i haven't grasped more than a slivered dessert slice of awareness
of half the invisible forces at play
in the benevolent mirage of it all
but i think—

____

Dancing

Ambient washes
Brief eye glimpses
Heart travel sketches
Forgetting outgrown shapes
New friends
Eyes closed, feeling
Sway

____

Symptom of space

Empty blank dots
Emptying further
Signalless cues
Rushing into

Subtle violences

A liberation of connection
Bringing us to realize it's better
Unconnected

An openness across space and time
Further complicating hearts and minds

____

Emotion Lite^{TM}

____

Evolving

Emotion transplant
She came up
Donor from a new land
A changing between two mutually exclusive bodies of wildly varying
temperatures
Stationary jet lag
This body is a zone
Emerge with an i
i to I
Lens focus, I
Wave sync, I
Walk into a dance
Gaining a sense of control, briefly
Winterspring in a larger cycle still

____

To the girl with the groovy energy

I hope you have an amazing night

A Way Home

Thanks to the mosquito for awakening me to think
Thanks to the strange dream putting my mind to work
With its familiar cast of old friends and coworkers, unknown place and
meanings

A way home was lying awake on the couch early that morning playing
through what arrived on that week of travel, and what was aspired to
come next down the tunnel
Trains, trains, more trains
Another day at a train station, what better setting for afterlife, and life yet
again
Petri dish of possibility parade
Dream aquarium
Dreams about luggage, wrong cars, misplaced vehicles
Dreams about former faces and personalities almost left behind
Dreams about conversations and strangeness
But never about what's to come; that oddly was left to the waking dream
Like an untouchable magic that even the wild miracle of the brain and
consciousness could not write in their mystical, vanishing inks
A way home was reflection
A way home was continuing into it all, feeling and following feeling
The eyes and smiles of others, dancing in other lands, finding the truth
bone and walking with it back to a foretold place heard by an inner ear
before this ever began

Some of the world's big cities seem to maze into their own identities. It's as if for each one, some auteur of time decided upon signature flourishes and casted them into a gargantuan fractal funhouse to replicate endlessly, alleyway begetting alleyway, building begetting building. Were this not true we would perhaps not be able to make such sarcastic remarks as, "We were at that one cafe in Amsterdam, you know, that one next to a canal and some bike lanes," or "Hey, remember that one bar in New York, kind of small, overpriced, had exposed brick and low lighting," or "We ate at that one diner in LA that was down the street from a retro-futurist building." To the foreign eye, the novel characteristics of each city in this tier seem to be so focal that they become magnified as a wallpaper casts throughout the city and our memories of it.

A readily apparent curse of this is that it can make it difficult to remember the exact name or location of 'that one Victorian in San Francisco we loved' or 'that pleasantly unpretentious bar in Berlin we went to that was near a kebab shop and a Späti, you know, that one,' when you next find yourself in that city (unless of course one is a checklist type tourist, frequenting only recognizable names that can be retraced through a travel blog, critic's column, or bookmark list). You may trial towards success, but oftentimes it seems to end up in a place you *think* is the one from the memory but after further inspection or sitting down you sadly realize is not the exact one you recall.

Frustrating as it may be, it seems in this discouraging factor also lies the beauty of such memories—the beauty in how it leaves something mysteriously untouchable, in another time, another realm, hidden in the city's replicating code, away from our present adult lives where we otherwise feel the creeping ennui of omniscient familiarity.

Seeing now that two separate pieces of art—a recent favorite song Bill LaMount's "Livin It Up" and an old favorite Frank O'Hara piece, "Having A Coke With You"—despite their disparate expressions, ultimately arrive at the same thesis.

The latter is a poem; the former is a poem sang over pensive yacht rock. Both take the audience through the author's journey to their dumbstruck realization—that art, travel, and indulgent pleasures are ultimately cheapened or vapid without an *other*.

Even now in a day half-submerged in the emotions of love's absence I can't help but wonder if both pieces overvalue alterity or humans' social nature while undervaluing the individual and their identity's relationship to the world which I think compounds and continues well throughout life, without need for other as compliment or completion.

In this regard I think Bill LaMount's work may have a more fully constructed realization in this sense. Where it seems O'Hara simply notes a realization (perhaps in relationship to his own craft at that time) that very achieved artists, sculptors, architects, etc. missed out on the joy and magic of romance and its shared and lived truth due to a presumed obsession with their art and its achievement, LaMount takes us through his pursuit of self and its ultimate endpoint—it's not all he imagined it to be, or rather that said pursuit only goes so far until one realizes there are perhaps more rich, honorable, evolving pursuits beyond one's own fantasies and personal checklists or ambitions.

———————————————

Neuro-linguistic Q: how do synapses, for a learned language that has not
been recently used, tie to episodic memory

———————————

golden wash, hand on tether still
child swinging in spring
then running excited to someone out of focus
yesterday, someone's jaw a'move, crooked on speed trying to flirt and find
another at 11am
a room outside the throb
she wanted to stay in paradise more
and met someone there who works in cryptocurrency
a loss of other
awake a little deeper it feel apart

that wasn't quite it

that wasn't quite it,

a dream in full black and white

Traced like rock texture
all over a body,

———————————

inevitable glass

you in the wrong ocean, traced in dream
stuck in sands' poor play
you look a stone and so you make as a jewel
so free and true a jewel all along
you say your parts are into one, a deep obsidian obelisk strong
and so they are, so you are
in making the idea towards inevitable glass,
through or mirrored unknown,
committing in time, the polish from erosion
you go to the obsidian mine for the milk bath of your dreams
and it's not; pale and dull, damp empty plain
a torture from smoothness, a breaking pain of truth
and you, a pupil's break, more under a lid's comforted pink
and you suddenly a plastic flower under glass
and you a psychology text's reduction, development and child thing
and the milk pains further from still being, itself
and the mine is a common field
and the mine is an empty room
and are you obsidian or are you glass

———————————————

the parable of the woman with glass
the parable of the woman with rope
the parable of the woman with a dream
the parable of the woman with herself
an education to escape flipped as a paper trap
inmate books, justice books, self-map books
strewn in paper strewn in document

I want the obsidian ornament surgery,
To be changed, to have it taken and put into me
Or to simply walk in the shop and
In a way that smells of knowledge and self say,
"I want the obsidian ornament surgery"

I long in arousal to exchange a currency for a metaphor of time
To walk outside after in a pain of satisfaction
having the shiny black new reflection inside of me
feeling the rest of my survival's acceptance of identity
like swallowing mornings after a thick dream or bad choice

The obsidian ornament is a place to put the emotion of hope
is a place to put the myth of the woman with the mysterious rope
is a place to put the postcard with the collectible-stamp of the smiling
foreigner who looks like everyone
is a place to put all the eyes that could quietly ask any differently
It moves emotion into alchemy, putting it into a word and book
Hiding in a pretty way with a fashion
A way to make myself more stone and make a stone more myself, a way
to lick the perfect and hold myself naked in the vacuum of a bigger idea
than death

And so I get it. I go into the shop and,
In a way that smells of knowledge and self, say
'I want the obsidian ornament surgery'
And they take me through the exciting passed down tradition
The paperwork, the cleaning of instruments and rapport-formation with
the operator

And they escort me back to the operating room where I lie down and
stare up at the artificial light like a new heaven, like hauntingly perfect
clouds outside of an airplane window moving from here to there
And like a god they place it into me, like a kiss, like a drop of liquid sugar,
like a private spaceship
And it is quiet and still and then it is over
We go back to the entry room and I thank them as a child to parents
And then it is time for another to receive some such operation so I exit
outside into a crude sun with the streets' movement all the same, bad
painting under spotlight, bar with the lights on
A dull malaise of the common
And all the busy people, even those of the obsidian, appear a bit uglier
I resolve to go to the stone garden to sing the song about growing
beautiful and memory
But I get there and the song sounds flat, made-up even,
So I stop, filling with the silence like a small vase, and I just sit
But too, I feel the stillness has turned on me, a broken cathedral for a lost
believer
I run my hand like a vehicle low on fuel over the site of change
and the smoothness is a dull torture, a breaking pain of truth.
The taste puts me on paper, dimensional, nostalgic
distributing me for walls or education in eternal repetition.
I'm suddenly a plastic flower under glass
In the flawed broken moment, I see myself finally, as obsidian.

Reminds me of years watching out for love

Reminds me of years spent watching out for love

Watching the lights go [final line]

I cast spells alone to the church of Imaginary
The community gave donations to it when I was younger
These days it's ignored with ivy swallowing it in greed
or else discouraged and torn down for new condos
Even the good
parts like a body's cells

I'm going to die someday too
And so feel hopeless and alive alone,
Invisibly sending the feel-good emotions like love and care, quietly
Radio tower blinks, distant cargo ship blips
From a bed in a room somewhere in a night

I recognize I may no longer have time to do this make-believe
participation when it is replaced with a catalog of people I share electrons
and food with, so I try to remember it consciously—
the still room with disappearing corners, the aloneness tasting
concurrently of autumn and apple,
the moon books, the silver dream of fish
The church survives on its own faith and change

———————————

I design a tattoo for the ghost of your backbone but I can't afford the postage to buy it
The world-drink puddles around my door, and I don't want to get my carpet wet

———————————

Our bodies are soft banks swallowing time until the quiet patrons revolt and tear it down to start something new
Our name and ideas are a meager branding

A body is a soft bank swallowing time

[or]

A body is a soft financial institution swallowing time
To yield more

———————————

Family of the void
Our common emptinesses
Were the bridges
Shapeless web
quiet links

And when one healed or solidified themselves
It erased the invisible for sake of making
The visible
Still yet, a response to the emptinesses

———————————

Feel better

———————————

Sorry, just saw this

———————————

Kindergarten - learn coding
First grade - write copy instead of sentences
Second grade - art class to develop :30 and :15 ad spots
Third grade - learn spreadsheets for costing out and assessing media
spend for ad from Second Grade
Fourth grade - practice writing professional emails
Fifth grade - learn history of fighting gov regulation as a business

____

Wait, what's greige?

____

angelfish, dog heaven, heart cookies   [good terms to use]

heart cookie of self
angelfishing for an okayness
passing the news all around this dog-heaven
with the idea that it may help the hypothetical symphony

[or]

heart cookie of self
angelfishing for an okayness
passing the news all around this dog-heaven
with the idea that it may help the peanuts, the paint-stained

Until it didn't, a bad gym. After all was said and done, it came down to a long correspondence over naturally threatening highway construction that ultimately couldn't be stopped. It's now so easily dismissed as a waste of time in hindsight. More lanes, more lanes, wider still, more. A bad gym grows. The glistening muscle under sweat, coursing with the unregulated supplement now too late to stop. Reagan tattoo burnt like from a branding iron. Watching everyone going to and from on the highway, ultimately home to envy the loved or look at their dog in envy. Imaginary games for survival, what else has gone. Are libraries still open? How small are the books in the even smaller section on how to decontaminate water? How confusing it is, the quiet water crisis underneath the leaking pollution of the highway. Exhaust is the operative idea here; exhaust and trying desperately to separate it from water. Anna and I had gone to a poetry reading a few months back. It was more of an open mic where everyone reads poetry; things open up like that. The caliber was what I imagine any of us could expect from such a thing, from ourselves I mean. Anyhow, I remember the degree of cringing, of pushing myself to listen to the readers and my physical response to them equally. One could posit ideas of recognizing a self or a past, and that's probably part of it, but I think it was all a communion of pain and embarrassment; it's helpful. Dogs still feel it and we soothe and love them after. After Anna and I left we talked about the degree of discomfort we felt, but quietly thought perhaps that's the airport wine-bar of it all, in any case. I walked home after even though I could've taken the train.

trying not to let the ape get up the attic stairs

____

psychic baggage

____

self-untitled

____

unmade self-things
which friends were under a similar cape shadow
which painted a money canvas in your way
who else with the moving sky or big explosion thoughts in likeness
and anyway, how much of a matter for each
you wonder alone again at home, where you feel you ought to be in any
case

____

looking at each other as we wanted to
light tossing
swallow my sculpture of time
or say it's molded to a verifiable liking
swallow my time of sculpture, all of us
becoming back in it
invisible graffitiers, where only
output remains, strange names following patterns
for people already at the end of time

———————————————

a dystopia future where we have to perpetually reinvent language
via double meaning in order to escape machine-learning/neoliberal
communication enterprises from effectively interpreting and categorizing
our language with each other

———————————————

I think the modern world makes it hard to live a truly ethical life.
The neoliberal forces, foreign real estate invasion on every side, and
consequentially needing to compromise one's morals and treatment of
their fellow person/the future of the world just to make enough to get
by. I don't like it. It's not punk rock, not even Christian, not even sexy, not
even beer with a friend to feel better. Another absurd human tendency,

how often now in order to be able to survive momentarily on this planet
we had to help destroy it.

———————————————

Men playing solitaire alone on their phones in subway-trains after work.

———————————————

a forbidden god

forbidden gods

———————————————

matters of different elegances ceramicists of different elegances you write
your way, i write mine, the clay is always sad, always real, everyone around
us on the street, alone, hungry, confused, damp

———————————————

psychedelics on the side

————————————

another mind
whose teeth bite a world-size eraser
branded with the words "that's not god"
who vigorously shakes back and forth
like a hammerhead shark
or broken amusement park ride

————————————

[flesh out the below]

i remember in childhood being cued in on another hidden piece of magic
in life.
Psst did you know about cooties?
Have you heard about Santa's list?
My friend's older brother told us about a pot of gold at the end of a
rainbow.
In this case it was about tunnels. Tunnels were like prayers.
-driving though tunnels holding breath you get a wish
-must've first discovered on a field trip or maybe when mom or dad
wanted my sister and i to be quiet for a few seconds
-i'd always wish for personal things, selfish things, the things we all want
early on in life before we understand more about it. - the house from

100

Blank Check, all the video games at Toys R Us, every lego, money. When
I was a little older more of the same—a certain girlfriend, to meet a
celebrity i like, a certain guitar, fame.
-though, overtime I tried to beat the game, outsmart it like people who
would ask a Genie for more wishes.
-sometime around late high school while reading Daniel Guérin and now
was able to drive myself through these tunnels, I recall wishing for class
war, wishing for the fall-out of the power elite.
-then, holding my breath less and less when driving through tunnels,
either losing hope, or busy trying to do something with its precursors

____

Friends on the sex trip
Just another way to short exit
Intermission everywhere
Intermission everything
And this time the play's ending
leads to something so entirely different
than the desired, simple reprieve of the rave's ending

____

Stop turning me into art
It's me
It's other
It's you,
Your little voice
Please stop recycling me
Into art for nothing better
Is that the right thing to do?
You already ask yourself

———————————

Like any 'successful' place
You begin to see the same faces there regularly
At first it's a check and balance
Then maybe a nice familial quality
Then eventually a questioning
Why are they here? Why am I here?
What does participation in any of this mean, at this point, for me, for others?
Is there a personal artisan brokenness I can't move beyond? They can't move beyond? What is that 'beyond'? Does it even actually exist, and are there better or healthier, more longitudinally sustainable ways to get there?

———————————

Practicing death
Pretending death
Taking our drugs and alcohol pretending death

———————————————

autographed e-reader
can you sign my kindl

———————————————

A near future where the middle- and upper-class start doing more
outlandish acts for pleasure; rates of recreational cheating skyrocket in
perfectly happy couples, intentionally life-threatening drug doses for
leisure, drunken free soloing, murder and suicide. All due to everything
else already getting consumed under experiential consumerism, so
the market and its psychological byproducts seek more novelty to
commoditize, disintegrating concept of polarized morality in sake
of consumption and ‚unique' experience as indicator of satisfaction
and social affirmation—outweighing fear and taboo, which become
progressively tranquil through mesmerizing velocitation of the consumer.

———————————————

You get harrowingly sad looking around at close friends seeing that
what was once their interesting opinionated personality has molded
itself into suddenly uninteresting manifestations of consumer identity.
A once rebellious friend impassioned by political criticisms and cosmic
ponderings is now a regurgitation machine who can only seem to utter
remarks on brands or where they and their partner traveled this quarter.
It wasn't the change of a friend and thus increasingly boring time
around a friend that was so frustrating as much as it was their shrugging
acceptance of it and therefore the suggested impending proliferation
of the phenomenon with others around you. And more so what that
indicates about humanity and identity at large. Things far greater than an
era seemed to be ending.

———————————

All the shut-down love potentials

———————————

Undo the spell

Texting his boyfriend on a cellphone. Undo the spell. A GIF brings mana,
a memory song brings luck, both just in case. A heart-feeling returning to
its real actual thingness

Leisurely pressure

A thought seems truer than idea
It is in the past, already experienced and done
Moons and satellites and great loves

After the ghost left

Bedrooms and Bathrooms

the new head of marketing is a doomer

---

the electronic producer's adolescent-parent relationship with the kick
drum

Pop-up Marxist fine-dining restaurant where each course is brought out
with a card showing transparent breakdown of costs incl. surplus value,
aiming to dispel the diners' commodity fetishism in real time.

---

dramatic lighting

---

pop song about being thirsty for your lover's ejaculate, called "Mineral Water"

———————————————

How much will „end of the world travel tours" cost? Will it even matter

———————————————

It overcame me again why I felt so awkward on Instagram, or why many of us feel perhaps a similar feeling when using proxy apps and sites for intimacy and dating, in that the human experiences and artworks which excited me and resonated to my core were those that were dismissed as imperfect. The low fidelity, the outsider artist, the child's seemingly abstract crayon drawing, the disposable camera photo of friends, the book of flawed yet maybe therefore more relatable poetry. Instagram meanwhile, as a marketing tool first and foremost, yielded human endeavor into a strife towards perfectionism and artifice. An emphasis on symmetry, doctored lighting, and staging self and experience in the likeness of commodity fetishism seemed to take favor over embraced blemish and humaneness. It was, in all matters of the term, sterile. A wasteland in a platonic cave, where the end of time is already reached and can be complacently sat in as long as one wishes; where one can see the majority of their friends, former colleagues, ex-partners, and loved ones tossing days of their life and one of its only true resources—finite time— like pieces of bread off a bridge, when that loaf of bread is all they have to last through the month.

Illegal time

eyes and ears can be convinced; the prime targets of advertising
nose and stomach are far wiser. pheromone and intuition are still yours.

if I had more time to shoot photos I would go around and solely take
photos of people in stores, the larger, the more commercially nauseating
or extravagantly, luxuriously fetishized, the better (though I suspect
department stores given the ubiquity and higher traffic would be much
more interesting and profound than high-end boutiques, zB). Because
it seems this is something that will no longer exist in the future, and
the current dismal timing of it all and seeing people still going into the
physical zones of malls and stores for the trance-like states to overcome
the present Zeitgeist seems to be the most unique.

everything is practicing dying
and you can practice purposeful dying
or you can practice purposeless dying
the former is an art
the latter is medicated amnesia

They were working hard
so they could buy clothes
to display to others that they have
a remedial understanding
of complementary colors and cycling trends

Girl outside Rewe shooting music video, correcting the PA - „it's not a
bridge, it's a pre-chorus"

Buying or receiving t-shirts as gifts almost always feels uncomfortable, I think because it's like giving a billboard to someone or fitting them into an identitary motto. And so if it's not exactly correct it feels, I think, forceful or reductive, as well as if someone close to you perhaps doesn't know you so well.

———————————

Agreeable outlines of playful violence

———————————

Beautiful machines, dutiful machines

———————————

Humans are such a thing of dreams
Such a thing of meanings and strife
That even when we habitually lay our bodies and actions down to end
each day
The dreaming and meanings and strife all continues to go about on its
own

———————————————

Ricardo Villalobos

The further away I got from techno
And a coaxing hypnosis of kick drums and novel melodies
The more I got back to kneeling at some weird altar of myself
Even my passions of music and dancing
From their backside,
From a rear view mirror on a camel heading now away from their
miraged oasis to something further in an unknown desert,
Now appeared clearer as releases against
capital, against market forces and frustration
I started reading in my armchair more
Staying in
Flirting less, seeking less novelty
Disoriented in new ways that felt better or somehow less bothered, truer

———————————————

In my German class filled with other transplants to Berlin
We learned vocabulary about the workplace
We discussed the cultural relativism of punctuality and were asked the
general length of lunch breaks within a full time job in our countries
We from the US answered the shortest amount-
Eating lunch at your desk or during a meeting.
What was that overused quote from the Dalai Lama - man overworks,
destroying his health, so he can afford to take care of his health?
It's like the majority of Americans would prefer to give their lives to
a corroding and endangering fiction rather than to the longevity of
themselves. I guess the post-enlightenment, like the evolution of Web 2.0,
was just a sad changing of the guard rather than a revolution.
An addict's switching of one fetish object to a new, more acceptable
one; Indiana Jones taking an antiquated treasure and replacing it with a
counter-weight, only to still get bulldozed by a giant boulder.

————————————

counting walls as our new primary creative mode

————————————

The world's ending but we can still go on vacation

————————————

Still life with McDonald's and bong

———————————

Ideas in light

———————————

Stuffed into a pocket of negotiation
You fit in their weekender-bag
In the memory vault
In the sale
In the commercial
In the book image
In the museum's third point,
In a weird triangulation with a past being perceived in a way that we
convince ourselves is the right way or the necessary way, more often than
just seeing it more as a past that stays in a museum

———————————

the escape from responsibility
the escape from decision
the escape from finitude

———————————

spontaneous assimilations with those who lick reality in the same degree
and dosage as you

———————————

the other side of fantasy

———————————

Character-based spiritual offenses

———————————

An age where people were educated enough to observe massive zeitgeist
changes in history and project about the same in the future,
And stupid enough to believe that they were correct

———————————————

I've never heard anyone say, "sitting still like a crazy person" only running
around.

———————————————

the slick scam

———————————————

Scared machine

———————————————

she told us:
"i realized either i could follow my ambition to an endpoint, perhaps
boringly albeit intensely
or i could throw myself abandon to drugs, and i chose drugs"
as she flicked the bag

When We Mean To Thank And Apologize At The Same Time

A Word For Concurrently Thanking And Apologizing

A word to say both thank you and I'm sorry

---

someone making art with a massive budget or spend from their ad
agency, while often impressive from a production and managerial angle,
typically fails to stir or impress me emotionally the way outsider-art
and creativity under the constriction of low budget and evasion of
commercial-appeal does.

Crowd-sourced assassination of Jeff Bezos

———————————

A sign on the door that says „only nice people and weirdos“

———————————

Sometimes the people are strangers, sometimes the people are friends

———————————

babysat by culture

———————————

an explanation of love where we are immaterial beings/energy/
recognition and the sensation we feel with each person with whom we've
had a strong connection throughout life was not something entirely due/
belonging to each of those material individuals but rather a singular
immaterial other who was leading us to experience them all.
Two immaterial soulmates pulling each other through their material
anchors through different experiences and relationships over time.
Nothing is lost.

———————————

In airbnbs with groups of friends
Taking warm wooden salad bowls out
And placing them on a large enough table
We commotion meanings out like toothpastes, pasta machines
We friendly pastel together
All oils and color combining,
Blending, complimenting, contrasting

———————————

Sometimes lost in an old city from previous times, before smartphones
when flaneuring was easier
How did I figure it out back then
I always ended up back where I needed to be after; how had I done it

I bent a picture of approximated possibility with someone I found attractive, like an unchewed stick of gum fresh out the foil, feeling it's hard contours progressively halving, fourthing, coming together and shaping into approximate forms as a flavor begins to reveal itself, for what duration I cannot say.

alone in truth

It takes me somewhere else, now
looking back briefly
I've lived a life of barely made trains.
Turned stones and last lights to turn off.
The final overhead reading lamp while the rest of the transatlantic flights
sleep, sore soles from being the sole soul to stay awake flâneuring through
unknown cobblestoned streets, just to see where they might lead. I've
been the one to kiss or run back to say one last thing to someone before
mutual disappearings; foreign loves, pursued dreams, written long notes
instead of short coolness; curious leaps and stories to share. Little sleep
and getting sick more often than those around me because of it, from
trying to do too much, seeing how stories end, in lived adventure and
bedside books.

I'm not insinuating some great life left unrealized by others, nor a "how-
to" to sell towards changing one's own. I think the age of that is in many
ways, hopefully, dead and gone. Maybe this is just an, 'It's possible,'
reminder to the type of person who might need to hear it, while there's
still time.

____

It's been nine years since I lived in that country, almost exactly to this week. I remember having a small dinner and kir to myself across from the Bataclan to see Explosions In The Sky live and crying, taking in my time of falling in love with a place. I remember Anna's cowboy boots, and the way her heels would click-clack, perfectly announcing the arrival of her vivacious presence. I remember countless espressi at that chain-café in the town. The blue of Lake Como while sitting on a lawn chair facing backward on a ferry one afternoon, weeks afterward.

———————————

Some of my favorite moments in life were spent alone in other places. Some of my favorite moments in life were spent alone in transit in other places.

———————————

lately I like sitting facing backwards on trains to pay more awareness and respect to everything that's left behind, and to appropriately acknowledge my blindness towards what may come in the future

———————————

Yeah whatever, pearls in rain
But to be more, in a way, yourself
Follow memory songs
Follow kindness
Not the chalice or tree to say
Trickery is a common sale
Longer trails an umbrella scheme
But ears to hearts, eyes to eyes
A diamond's dream of what
A diamond could've been
No one ever sells mud
No one ever sells the free part of a dinner with friends
No one ever sells a real mountain chair
So uh
Here, be a quiet bar-gum, dumb-dumb
See ya

———————————

Here in the small, old town
where the all restaurants remain in the same place
Maybe time is still a friend
I should call them tomorrow

———————————

We all die young
don't buy the video
all the same in graphite,
all the same in stream

———————————

Heavy rounds

———————————

The big crazy calm-down

———————————

From Babylon to Avalon

———————————

The way people colloquially say 'That's the spirit,' as if acknowledging
something bigger revisiting or awakening through us in a moment

——————————————

Passing through and passing on

——————————————

give me rides and ridges,
strips and stripe,
shapes that morph
into something else

——————————————

I got locked in the stairwell of a coworking space
that my friend had membership at
as I was trying to exit during afterhours
It felt like an appropriate metaphor, or materialization of my headspace
a comedic fake-trap created by reluctant participation in neoliberalism

ideas as ultimate organisms in reality; the survival of ideas over generations of humans—their meat containers, helping the ideas' evolution and survival

sometimes I wonder what it feels like to be one of those people whose highlight experience in life was a large-production viral video where they propose to someone

editing old poems written in moments of clarity
now seeming so obvious, often trite, and this will be the same i'm sure
trying to get something out, to reach and complete or better,
i think anything good has happened on its own, a chance chosen by time
then it's gone and something continues; like finishing a book and not too long after
going to the shelf for another. leaving a loved one at an airport or a train station
and there's still the journey ahead to change you before you even get to the place first intended
getting a job or an acceptance letter and really it's how you feel years later when you leave;
what i mean to say by this, as i've readopted my old writing style from editing so much of it today,
is that i think the book never mattered.
the book, jukebox, only happened to show me it doesn't matter,
to serve as a decoy to get me to where i needed to go for something else.
a MacGuffin, like anything outside of human connection,
and I think expressions and creations, being so earnestly close to it,
in their desperate though still often admirable attempt, are so easily mistaken for it.
the book was already a time machine, a transporter for me. each piece
added up moved me through countries, stages, jobs, dreams, realizations,
to be here in Berlin now where I finish it and then leave it to have a life
of its own. to have a life of my own and take a new direction.

---

it made me happy to think of how Reddit was replacing other forms of social media which tended to highlight the user more, whether by keeping their individualized thoughts isolated in a stream, providing user photos and bios, or accompanying blue check marks. Reddit appeared to be returning to the forum era of the internet where the importance seemed more kept on a topic, evolving an idea as a community, rather than evolving the owner of an idea through associated value, affirmation, or attack as seemed more the case on venues like Facebook and Twitter.

I remember boarding a flight from Kathmandu to Bangkok after learning the news about Mark Hollis. Listening to an online radio dj's mix of songs from his career as I watched people exiting and boarding flights on the tarmac. Thinking I may not necessarily have much long to go either. It felt like a brief link, a connecting airport to an afterlife.

---

falling in love at the end of the world
like it wasn't that way all along
as if it wasn't that way all along
ends to ends, do you want another glass?
yeah, I think I might have one
so what i mean is,

————————————————

Also your smile is perfect

————————————————

a bed for a chaotic world

————————————————

Feeler

————————————————

broken castle of cereal bowls and moving screens

————————————————

128

local radio pop songs felt like a hearse
painted around the two of us waving away the idea of a couple's
caricature drawing
the cardiologist told you breeding hopes are on a receipt or a script
for the romantic drama that the world had lost its dream over

———————————————

another great fake relief
another great fake relief
i got ambition for a couch,
comfy water-sports and sleeping systems,
for a way to shrug a small rock

———————————————

we met at a garage sale and you said i should go to the store instead
when you carry around tubs of the wrong things
you remind me i should've gone to the store instead
but either way i might soon be out of money
or just tired of having things that'll get donated again anyways

———————————————

The friendly upperclassmen

---

boredom machines

Someone upstairs keeps spitting out the window
So I put a paper pot out on the doorstep

Apocalyptic Angst

---

all the brown liquors in hell

Lottery winners wanting to defend the slot machine's lot
But were never quite sure which holy book explained how it works
Just morally bankrupt men lined up
In banks before the rapture ruptured their subcutaneous oil lines

World War 3 draft is where dude pass me a corona
turns into dude pass me the corona virus

another cam show to pay student loans

another cam show to lonely overworked men
to pay her way out of a useless MBA

6 Life-Hacks On How To Go Fuck Yourself
WikiHow: To Go Fuck Yourself
My Ted Talk On Why TedTalks Should Go Fuck Themselves
Medium Post: We Should All Go Fuck Ourselves
MUA Tutorial: Easy Guide On How To Get That Go Fuck Yourself
Look
PUA Tutorial: Easy Guide On How To Get Women To Tell You To Go
Fuck Yourself
Cosmo's 101 Ways To Spice Up Telling Your Man To Go Fuck Himself
Men's Health's 101 Ways To Get Those Go Fuck Yourself Abs
Reddit AMA: I Previously Went And Fucked Myself, Now Want To Help
Others Go And Fuck Themselves
Jordan Peterson OWNS Popular Personality With Pseudo-Intellectual
Argument About How Going And Fucking Ourselves Cleans Our Rooms
Zizek's Film Analysis About How Gigli Was About The Class Struggle
Against Going And Fucking Ourselves
Joe Rogen Passively Agrees With Controversial Guest Misinforming The
Audience About Whose Behind Us Going And Fucking Ourselves
Video Of Famous Gamer Personality Telling Strangers On Fortnite To
Go Fuck Themselves
LinkedIn Notification: Congratulate Your Loosely Based Connection On
Their New Position Where They Get To Be More Central To The Action
Of Going And Fucking Themselves

The investors found a time machine

Investors in a time machine

He had to leave after the blowjob
To get to to the VC's office and
watch porn in the bathroom before his pitch:
An app for prop-bets on the drones in WW3

some days making a perfect bean water is the only hope i need

ruining the world still with the extinct-animal extractors
can i shrug it away, can we shrug it away, i don't think so

the television music coordinator for the NFL,
sighing his way home on a bus
the copywriter for the tech company,
helping the noble businessmen seduce the world
has no time after 60 hours to seduce or be seduced in her own
the C-suite man for the forgettable brand,
not even in it for the tesla or airline points
just trying to finish the mortgage and get the kids through college;
no time to surf anymore

———————————

mother with a bedtime story app to lullaby her first born
so she can use her wine delivery app while the earth's torn

———————————

Quoting forgotten ideas

———————————

Making an impostor celebrity account for a master's thesis

____

selecting 'remind me later' on computer update notifications
as a way to simultaneously regain my control in delaying accelerationism
and feel the guilt of procrastinating on solutions as we've all done in this
lifetime

____

bad memory foam

____

political sadness's parallax

____

more mutated mp3 paintings

more mutated rap paintings

wasted rap battles

desperate color

DJ Krankwelt
DJ Consumer Identity Connection

time still drizzling out from the leaking vault of eternity—
a moonlit river for the animals to still go to, to meet and survive a little
further

---

deepfake poems

---

love torrent

P2P alternatives

---

mere transport materials for the ideosphere

---

lacto-ferments but for ideas

---

the camera lens made us invent it

Market corrections were going through a market correction

Market corrections
Ideals were lying,
Fictionalism's pragmatism got bankrupted by reality's tax,
and so it corrected the inflated images of market corrections

---

The perfect customer is a mostly, but not entirely, miserable one

---

In a hotel skybox, sleepless next to a love, moving my mind over futures
like a hand over a ring of keys, trying to feel out the right one

———————————————————

quiet thinking in my apartment alone, i look at my plant that i'm taking
care of
and my heart projects a you-feeling between its shapes, as i wonder where
you are
and see the ways we could be growing together.

———————————————————

Sculptures in light
Sculpting in light

———————————————————

This was a year for clearing the cache

———————————————————

I download all of Donald Fagen's solo albums
and think twice about if I should get more tattoos on the next vacation,
how a guy talking about Fagen's solo albums in an online forum once wrote
that he likes one because it tells road-trip stories; I read some
and they sound like itching for drinks and romantic ideas and everything
else under the 'partying' umbrella; I wonder about people I've seen doing
that into old age
how sometimes it looks weird and sad, not because the age, but because it
appeared
that they were on the ride for too long, just another rotation
I think of that Bat For Lashes song, "Laura" about staying in the party
while friends move on
I think about the conversation an ex had with me over social media
recently about the old
"passion vs. pragmatics/ease" dichotomy in relationships, and if it leaves
any boat in a favorable position
and I haven't even started listening to the Donald Fagen solo albums yet

————————————

At a friend's birthday and we enter a bar with an opening room playing
Steely Dan. It's 2020. it's all over.

————————————

All of us finding each other in this crazy world, in the spinning strings of
its music's messages

———————————

Sending photos of material things that the other person enjoys as a way
to still connect with them

———————————

When you close your eyes a space is created

———————————

Worlds that were never there
so many people chasing worlds that were never there
to the point that they lose this one

———————————

Bad ending

———————————————

a natural wine producer named : 'blood of the billionaires who we
rightfully murdered during the revolution'; offerings include 'vengeance,'
'best served cold,' 'no sympathy for mr. bezos,' 'musk's dead musk,'
'branson's virgin flesh,' 'ice pick ice wine'

———————————————

actors, directors, musicians, etc. bringing out a stack of books, films, or
albums on their late night talk show interviews and instead of promoting
their work, they shine light on the works of others that inspire them, esp.
lesser known talents who lack such platforms, a creative and kind way to
pay it forward that I haven't seen done before in such venues

———————————————

pill reports

dead man's pill report

it's poignant that "free" in english can infer both *without being controlled* and *without having a cost*, as compared to in german, which has separate terms "frei" vs. "kostenlos/umsonst" ; that a desirable state of economics is used to describe people and human rights in the angloworld.

culture's not a friend

still stranging
some times better than others
better at leaving math problems unfinished
better at dull pencils
like flowers around the house,
bought just because.

"Unstable, unavailable, unreliable. I am my wifi connection…" she said.

---

church full of cities

---

kapital punishment

---

we wanted to fuck conveniently, instead we got fucked by convenience

---

selfies continued reeling like a parade of drunken crying
the television kept glowing like a vacant museum exhibit
my friend working in health insurance kept playing golf
a dog barked somewhere

———————————

heartbreak ikebana

———————————

a spelling bee of ghosts

———————————

"marconi plays the marimba"

———————————

sterilize your tears

———————————

karmic compatibility

———————————

capitalistic communes of the future

———————————

Stoned, with a movie

———————————

worried completionists seeking the discog of experience
to cry in a private library in some near faraway cemetery

Latent content producers
the more secrets you create, the lonelier you feel.

The only noun I like is: verbs

I fish through a night of finally going back out again
Strips and streamers
A weird gold weaves, away from the rest
Appearing
Strange safety
To do obviously, deserving an other

karaoke tattoos

____

modest stirrings

____

lost in the fridge

____

the inheritance; the savior
reaching outside of agency

____

bumping into old faces around heaven

but we're already at the afterparty…?

Elaborate traps

foundational misunderstandings on the semantics and contours of the
word "freedom"

a very long street where everyone is reading copies of The Great Gatsby
and crying

Caves and grottos

———————————————

the things we thought would heal us but didn't

———————————————

ultimately incorrect answers

———————————————

two people fucking with very bright headlamps on

———————————————

Distractive reconstructions

The theatrics of Dirty Dancing

Outsourced fantasies

why'd she pick her particular pornstar name
we used to do g and coke in LA hotel parties
that i'd walked into, thinking to myself
"i'm becoming a bret easton ellis novel if i don't get out of this city"
soon after i did, and she stayed, always with eyes
saying something that felt learned and artificial
like a good portion of the city, in aspiring role

there was never anything between us
a lot of eye contact, likely from being so different
one time i remember asking her what her dream was
she mentioned new york without strong conviction,
just that she had always wanted to go there, she liked it there

or the time, late at a new years eve warehouse rave
off of a few pressed pills and cheap champagne,
making out with a portion of the room and then confronting her
and asking point blank who she actually was, why was she so secretive and
stored in eyes and eyebrows
answers of Jumbo's transitioned into escorting as of late, but don't tell
anyone
i didn't. nor did she, just eyes continuing
afterwards whenever we saw each other in that group of partiers.

the only time we talked after i left the city
was when she messaged me asking about some self-help book i shared on
instagram
i wanted to ask her if she ever made it to new york,
maybe i already had earlier, but if so she never replied, for whatever
reason

today i thought of checking in, in the way you sometimes do just to see if
someone made it out alright
i went to her profile and saw
a linktree to onlyfans and brazzers for a name I didn't recognize

i wondered why she picked it,
like the eye contact, or the few confiding sentences she ever let out
under the effect of the time, and Los Angeles;
a last crumb of sincerity prior to perpetual molding into a brand,
steamrolling charade or indifference,
all the same. i was no better on the other side of it.

anyway, it looked like she was doing fine.

———————————————————

Heather's new pill

————————————————

She hauled her loneliness around the world with her.

————————————————

I trick my brain with some things it doesn't need

____

Bad compression

____

Rebrand "editing" and other post-production processes as "hauntological negotiations"

____

to better illustrate oneself through acquired matter
to better reveal the internal through externally associated matter

____

the era of the empty gesture

____

we aren't made sad by the same things
but it works all the same

____

fake blonde

____

hobbyist

____

a country of perpetual amnesia

____

and all of it, for the wrong goal

———————

the best consumer

the one who consumes best

———————

after no one wants to play anymore
it's just the lonely boy remaining in the empty world

———————

If money wasn't green

———————

Up and down the stairs

responsible aging partiers

Camouflaged lonelinesses

So many were concerned with what they were or what they could briefly
acquire through contracts before death. He became attracted to people
who were more focused on what they were doing, people who recognized
that we were all just meager short-term loans of energy. Some spend their
lives trying to fit the nature of a noun or attract adjectives, to be a subject,
to acquire objects, or stay in the ties of prepositional phrases. Others
seemed to recognize that such pursuits only seem to slow down our
actual nature, our power of doing, contributing, as brief verbs.

you'll need the others like a card after the river
except now the green table's only aligned with helpful machines.
another drink? asks yet another, appearing from behind you, neither
suddenly nor comfortingly.

somehow there's still smoke clearing in the foreground, even now,
but there's no more visors, no more sunglasses or grinning
games, because what's the point?

it'll still be announced and broadcasted, we still need that
in some sad and comical way, like a comeback vegas victory
on live television, played by someone you'll never meet
as you down another beer at the local bar, secretly rooting for them as if
it were everything.

in the best case, it makes you get up before it ends
to call a bookie out of misguided aspiration, or better yet, to call any of
the others, just to say hello and contribute
[alt: just to say hello and crease]

———————————————

looking up a purchasable t-shirt for something prior to fully consuming
the thing itself
and even so, why then?

———————————————

the wrong rewards

———————————

different sameness makes the same difference

———————————

Jesus's favorite country

———————————

portrayals

———————————

church builders like to think they're building something for the future
but it's always for the past

alt: church builders like to think they're building something to free the future
but it's always to entrap in the past

———————————————

Lesbian liberal cheerleader at Tennessee Titans game

———————————————

they just wanted to enjoy it a little further

———————————————

liked how it looks but not how it feels

———————————————

New software for old hardware

---

endless theater

---

bio-feedback, bio-distortion

The spirit vanishes

---

all the front-facing camera videos on social media from friends and family
who have hundreds of followers or less
illustrates how we've further gone into the positivistic rule of post-
surveillance psycho-politics (b. han).
the language, mirroring that of high-earning social media personalities,
exemplifies such:
"hey guys, so today I wanted to show you how I make [x]"
"some of you may have noticed I haven't been on here for awhile"
"if you like this, feel free to follow along on my journey on [platform]"
the movement of the everyperson into encapsulating a platform-capitalist
celebrity and the respective spirit of entrepreneurialism to an audience of
mere friends, family, and romantic interests as if they were their fans or
consumers
further accepts and integrates us into the role of such.

———————————

A memory of when I was living in France in 2011 and a local friend
remarked about how people found it funny how a lot of America's "Food
Network" wasn't depicting chefs preparing food but rather people going
to restaurants and eating food.

And now over the past few years some of the highest performing content
on YouTube is videos of people unboxing purchased products, videos of
people reacting to other peoples' videos, videos of people reading other
peoples' tweets, Korean mukbang videos, videos of other people playing
video games. Pornography's placement of the audience is becoming
proliferated through other hyper popular content. We're progressively
more and more voyeuristic in our digestion of consumption-oriented
entertainment. The act of consumption is performed for both the
subject's and direct object's consumption interchangeably. It is rapidly

becoming less of us watching someone else, and more, becoming our possessed consumption consuming others' consumption.

Fittingly, something similar appears to be taking root when it comes to another type of currently popular content—the large surge of remakes and cultural nostalgia porn in our era of late-capitalism. When we imbibe these films we are psychologically consuming the consumption of the earlier self at their moment of the first encounter. Jung talked about how when we feel a strong powerful connection with a piece of art—a tableau in a museum, a live rendition of a piece of music, a film, a book—it is our unconscious and the unconscious of the artwork's creator reaching out and embracing each other, in recognition. Thus if we feel some way about a piece of art (maybe generous of a term at times) that is over-the-top in its overt calling-back of a more memorable preceding piece of art, such as in the case of a late sequel or reboot, then how much is our unconscious reaching out to this new art, vs. reaching out to a prior state of our unconscious—how much are we consuming this new piece, versus holding it up to the hope that we might be consuming our previous self's consumption of the original piece. Our consumption is extending beyond object and consumer, and moving further into degrees of consuming another consumer's consumption, or we are purchasing admissions that unspokenly sell us the possibility to consume previous versions of ourselves in a way that feels escapistly novel and infallibly potent. Being sold one's own self, one's prior experience, as drug.

―――――――――――――

If exponentially less original ideas exist at a level of cultural awareness as time progresses, then over time we move consumption into progressively higher degrees of consuming the past, the already known or previously experienced—certainly in terms of a collective unconscious at least. We consume consumption and byproducts of previous consumption more than any actual products themselves.

———————————

if ideas are larger organisms or viruses merely moving through human beings, like life-extending vessels to ensure their survival over time and space, then a human's choice to live in a certain area comes down to a decision of graveyards. all a culture is, is a collection of hanging specters, thus a selection to live in one culture or another is a decision of which haunted house to marinade in, which petri dish of psychological biota we wish to ferment in, and with, overtime.

———————————

Sims, simps, and simulacra

———————————

Everything in life is a fight against the past, a long process of intensive communal therapy in order to free ourselves and one another, to build a better future.

____

When you strip away all cleverness what do you have left to communicate? *That* is it.

____

Talking with a friend about aging, future plans, diminishing returns, getting old. They say they feel like they're getting further along on the branch of a tree; where fewer and fewer routes are available before the end point. His analogy seems elegant. When you're young you're at the source, the root, all courses are open and in front of you; over time you get further up the tree, and consequently have less and less options and possibilities ahead.

____

Idea dealer

———————————————

playing games with everyone's attention,
playing games with everyone's time

———————————

Broken summoners
Trying to call light to their privacy
To haunt into a moment's freedom
In exchange for lost time

———————————

xerox'd champagne

———————————

The massage museum
Hung between the frozen rain

Reluctant businessmen

Most of the good shit in life thus far seems to have come from moments of simply asking "where is it all going?"

Look in the mirror when you're stoned

A little quieter now

"can I use this time to say something?"

———————————————

gimbal feat. dongle

———————————————

incompatible futures

———————————————

Renaming casual cancel-culture and IdPol warranting as "mutually agreed upon choices to stay in the Vampire Castle"

———————————————

false control

____

The strangeness of how we scream codified versions of "help me escape" during our most intimate shared intimacies

____

doubting existence

____

she would watch pressure washing and blackhead-removal videos on YouTube to de-stress after overworked days

____

An ornate absence

____

reincarnatal lag

---

everyone getting spat out at the various end inertia points of
psychological repetitions; gravitational slingshot from ringing around
psychic black holes

---

plastic surgery for the gods

---

the cost of anything is the amount of mortal time, and thus trust, you're
willing to put into it, perpetual kierkegaardian leaps of faith, imposed
against both imminent omnipresent death and a sun that will eventually
explode and melt any sort of materialism or legacy that one could leave
behind. the point is, nevertheless, the exercise under such conditions, and
what and who that brings us to.

what movies did I lend him in the dream…

Ugly ceiling color

[or]

Suddenly ugly ceiling color

what if resting or exerted force in existence works in a concurrently macro and micro way, like reflexively or I guess too, refractively? like two fractals passing in opposite directions; one descending while the other ascends, yet both maintaining present action in the same moment.

if the actions and choices we make at the full top-down level, are, in some sort of other concurrent reality or dimension, influential in a bottom-up process. as if we're occupying top-level managerial positioning in our own life, and concurrently low-level productive action at a cellular level for another, unbeknownst to us at the same time. not just philosophically/ ethically, as proposed by the Kantian categorical imperative, or the Sartrien talk about how we must be the lawmakers (from, I think, Existentialism Is A Humanism), but too at a bio-materialistic via quantum-mechanical level through quantum non-locality.

if somehow through quantum non-locality or through nonlinear displacement of energy within a system, we might be both simultaneously the conscious of our perceived self (a full body, "full human" life) and also, dimensionally, an operative cell in another.

———————————————

Outsourcing our emotions to emojis

———————————————

is the self that recalls a previous experience the true self since it's
remarking upon what it has already absorbed and integrated, or is it as
malleable as the present, fluid self that merely exerts and acts, processing
in half-action, realizing its absorbed implication later in identitary lag?

Acknowledgments

First, it goes without saying, but I'd like to acknowledge and thank the same people in my life from the Acknowledgments section of my prior book. Additionally, I'd like to give a shout-out to Madison Bible who went on that Picasso-exhibit date with me in college (if you ever read this, I hope you're doing well and that you were able to win the lotto and get your dad that sports car). Also, a thank you to the Seattle Art Museum and all other museums, gallery spaces, community centers, and cafés that continue to showcase works possessing what might be considered *incomplete* or *imperfect* qualities. A thank you to the cities and participating venues in things like First Thursdays or art-walk nights that help make local exposure to art more accessible regardless of socioeconomic status, gate-keeping, or class; being able to encounter a variety of art forms, styles, practitioners, and approaches, especially at a young age, is vital. Biggups to all of the outside-artists and imperfect creators of the world. To a former coworker, Reid Backstrom whose doodles I always enjoyed seeing in the office. To a former classmate from high school, Gannon Reedy, whose doodles have also brought a smile to my face when I would see them on social media. To my friend Robby Hart who has possessed an admirable, sustained curiosity and willingness to try his hand at new modes of creative expression ever since I've met him. To former bandmates or friends who I've jammed with, from high school to the present: Conrad Nichols, Ryan Melnick, Mike Bulanti, Alex Vlahov, Cam Schultz, the aforementioned Robert Hart, Dan Ferraro, and Nathalie Capello. A tremendous thank you to the magazine *mono.kultur* for its outstanding curation of vantages into creators from various disciplines. To Brian Eno, a personal hero of mine, and to *mono.kultur*'s published interview between him and his daughter, Irial Eno, which was not just a big influence on this book but also remains one of my favorite interviews that I've ever read.

To people doing it just for the fun of it, or simply because they need to get it out of them and into the world. To a creator in Kyiv, who was asked by a painter acquaintance in Berlin why she creates, to which she replied, "Creating is the only thing valid." Fair degree of truth there. To childhood teachers and art camp volunteers, for giving youth the space and support to freely explore themselves creatively without high stakes or expectations. To friends and acquaintances who've started party series, labels, bands, zines, publications, and other creative projects for the sake of positive momentum, if not the sole reason of: "Why not?"

Prior to COVID, I was traveling a fair amount during the time of this book's entries, thus it would be an oversight to not thank the many generous and helpful workers of the global travel industry. To the beautiful and kind people whom I've met during these travels, including those who I now consider some of my best friends. To the places in which I've lived and the ability to explore them; to walks alone, flâneurism, dérive, and other related concepts and practices which remain crucial for my ability to let the mind wander so that it can experiment and make disparate connections. Additionally, a thank you to all who helped pitch, create, and develop Apple's *Notes* application, and to those who help maintain it today.

One or two handfuls of the entries from this book came to me during hikes alone on low doses of psilocybin, something I've found to be very beneficial to my relationships with myself and the world over the past few years. Thus I would like to give a shout-out to Timothy Leary and other early pioneering researchers who helped put psilocybin on the map, to those who currently make this beneficial plant available in their communities and treat it with the respect it deserves, to the Multidisciplinary Association for Psychedelic Studies (MAPS), and to everyone else involved in researching, fundraising, lobbying, and working for the approved clinical use, reduced classification, and decriminalization of this sacred and healing compound around the world. Also a big thank you to all who help maintain the trails, nature reserves, and parks of the world. To the friendly, stray Tibetan dogs who provided some companionship on an important and healing hike in Nagarkot.

To the many amazing, inspiring creators and creative works whose rough-around-the-edges approach or general embrace of the imperfect has left a mark on me, and subsequently influenced the release of this book. Notably: J Dilla, Robert Pollard, Tobin Sprout, Pavement, Martin Newell, The Velvet Underground, Brian Eno, The Clean, The Fall, Sebadoh, Elliott Smith, Ariel Pink, Matt Fishbeck, R. Stevie Moore, Vini Reilly, Bill Callahan, D'Angelo, Questlove, Liz Phair, Triple 6 Mafia, DJ Screw & the Screwed Up Click, Lil B, Minor Threat, James Ferarro, Dean Blunt, Sam Mehran, Daniel Lopatin, Swirlies, Harry Merry, Bobb Trimble, Bob Desper, Nikki Sudden, Billy Childish, Mark & Clive Ives, CocoRosie, Owen Ashworth, E. E. Cummings, Jack Keroauc, Allen Ginsberg, William S. Burroughs, Lawrence Ferlinghetti, Walt Whitman, Frank O'Hara, Charles Bukowski, Foxes In Fiction, Donnie & Joe Emerson, Death, Walter Hawkins and the Love Center Choir, Pastor T. L. Barrett & the Youth For Christ Choir, Phil Elverum, Calvin Johnson, Kimya Dawson, Adam Green, Jeffrey Lewis, Miranda July, Peach Kelli Pop, Neutral Milk Hotel, Elephant 6 Records, K Records, Awful Records, Flying Nun Records, Les Disques Du Crépuscule, Music From Memory, Kranky, Melody As Truth, Stroom, Cordelia Records, Sex Tags, Janushoved, Hippos In Tanks, Bright Eyes, Todd Rundgren, The Shaggs, Dunkelziffer, Black Dice, Merzbow, Xiu Xiu, Fred Welton Warmsley III, Minutemen, Ty Segall, Thee Oh Sees, Gucci Mane, Steve Hiett, Mike Polizze, Molly Nilsson, John Maus, Wesley Willis, Lewis, Zoviet France, Nate Grace, Jessie Jenkins, Guitar Wolf, Les Rallizes Dénudés, Daniel Johnston, Alex Zhang Hungtai, John Darnielle, Liz Harris, Henry Darger, Mogu Takahashi, Lawrence, Omar S, Lobster Theremin, Chris Marker, Daido Moriyama, Saul Leiter, Peter Doig, Richard Haines, 100% Orange/Kenji Oikawa, Tobias Jesso Jr., Braulio Amado, Stefan Marx,

Richard Clifford Diebenkorn Jr., Alejandro Jodorowsky, John Cassavetes, Jim Jarmusch, Apollonios's *Belvedere Torso*; punk, ambient, DIY, Italo, the Japanese noise scene, C86, grime, jungle, chopped & screwed, Memphis rap, lo-fi hip-hop, lo-fi house; the Atlanta rap scene for their prolific output and peerless work ethic; zine culture, xerox art, art made by children, community projects, and the creative night-and-weekend-warriors of the world. Additionally, a thank you to the beautiful work, ethos, and spirit of Friedensreich Regentag Dunkelbunt Hundertwasser.

To the palm-reader with the intense eyes at the *Almost Magazine* (FKA *Almost 30 Magazine*) release event at Do You Read Me Berlin? in 2019, for telling me it was time to connect with others again—you were right, thank you.

And lastly, my acknowledged appreciation and apologies to anyone who has patiently waited after I've obnoxiously said, "Wait, sorry, I need to quickly write something down in my phone," and a thank you for the respective ideas or associations that each had provoked.

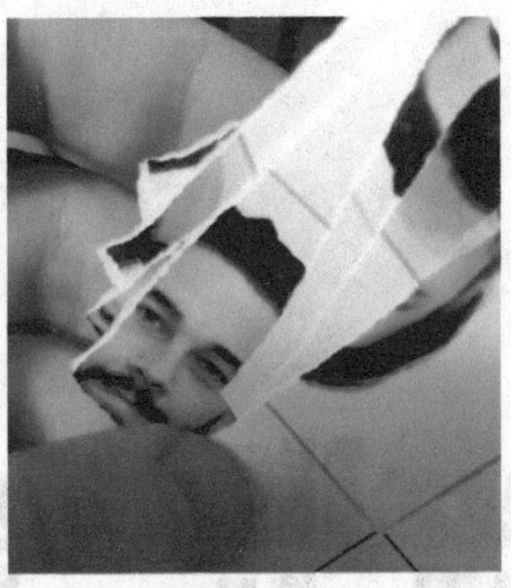

Notes App is Matt Brand's second book. Originally from Redwood City, California, the author has spent his adult life in Seattle, Grenoble, Los Angeles, San Francisco, and Berlin. He prefers verbs over nouns, life-long amateurs over professionals, and face-to-face interactions over digital proxies. He believes that humans are inherently good despite our capacities to get misled or under-nurtured in our psychological development.

Matt's writing tends to orbit around hauntology and the human condition under late-capitalism via themes such as spectacle, intimacy, splintering individualism, isolation, and self-delusion. He hopes that putting such focuses on creative display might serve to aid others' reflection and self-awareness—to help comfort the afflicted and afflict the comfortable, as the saying goes. Currently, when not writing or working on releases, Matt is trying to assess the best routes forward for contributing to sizable dual-power and material change. He is always open to connecting with others who are trying to do the same.

Qualitative Methods

www.qualitative-methods.com
@qualitative_methods